CHAPMAN
TRAILERING

The Complete Guide to Pulling,
Parking, Launching, & Retrieving
Your Boat

.

CHAPMAN
TRAILERING

The Complete Guide to Pulling, Parking, Launching, & Retrieving Your Boat

JOE SKORUPA & PAT PIPER

Hearst Books

A Division of Sterling Publishing Co., Inc.

New York

Skorupa, Joe.
  Chapman trailering : the complete guide to pulling, parking, launching & retrieving your boat / Joe Skorupa & Pat Piper.
      p. cm.
  Rev. ed. of: Hearst Marine Books trailerboat guide / Joe Skorupa. 1993.
  Includes index.
  ISBN 1-58816-459-4
  1. Boat trailers. 2. Boats and boating. I. Piper, Pat, 1953- II. Skorupa, Joe. Hearst Marine Books trailerboat guide. III. Title.
  TL297.2.S43 2005
  688.6—dc22   2005013112
  10 9 8 7 6 5 4 3 2 1

Published by Hearst Books
A Division of Sterling Publishing Co., Inc.
387 Park Avenue South, New York, N.Y. 10016

CHAPMAN and CHAPMAN PILOTING and Hearst Books are trademarks owned by Hearst Communications, Inc.

For information about custom editions, special sales, premium and corporate purchases, please contact Sterling Special Sales Department at 800-805-5489 or specialsales@sterlingpub.com.

Distributed in Canada by Sterling Publishing
c/o Canadian Manda Group, 165 Dufferin Street
Toronto, Ontario, Canada M6K 3H6

Manufactured in China

Sterling ISBN 13: 978-158816-459-9
ISBN 10: 1-58816-459-4

Contents

Introduction

 THERE ARE MORE THAN SEVEN MILLION BOAT trailers in the United States right now. And because you have this book in your hands, that number might be about to increase. As slip fees and moorings at marinas continue to become more and more expensive, more boaters are choosing to arrive at the water with their boats in tow.

When this book was first published in 1993, there wasn't an aluminum trailer to be found. In some states, laws for boat trailers were non-existent. Access to the water wasn't talked about. A lot has happened since that time. Taking your boat down the street to the local ramp or to another state is still an enjoyable way to spend time with friends and family. But now there are more boaters. And with this increase, you've probably heard many of your fellow trailer boaters talk about the need for some kind of exam prior to going on the water. In fact, most states are now requiring boat operators to complete successfully some kind of basic boating skills class before the boat is even registered. As a result, it's all the more important to have an understanding about your boat and trailer and how to keep a safe distance not only on the road but in the water too.

In the pages to come, the basics of trailer boating are explored—from the boat and trailer and tow vehicle individually, to how they all work together in taking you from Point A to Point B and back again. Along the way, you'll be introduced to areas where problems can occur so that you'll be able to anticipate things that can—and sometimes will—go wrong. With this knowledge and some time on the road with your boat in tow, you are going to be able to go boating safely and efficiently anywhere there's a launch ramp.

Each chapter concludes with some points to keep in mind, and throughout this book, you will come across points that have been made before. We aren't going to apologize for repetition. It's important. And too many boat owners are on the road—and the water—without a clue about basic maintenance and operation. You're not going to be among them.

Unfortunately, it happens again and again that boats, trailers, and tow vehicles are sold every day without any explanation whatsoever by dealers or salesmen of what to expect or how things actually work to people intending to spend a day with friends and family on the water. A well-worn boat trailer story is based on this very situation:

> *A man buys a boat and trailer and takes his new equipment to the local boat ramp where he launches and heads out on the water. With an eager thrust of the throttle, he accelerates to see how the boat performs but is dismayed when it struggles to get up on plane. Disgusted, he turns around and heads back to the boat ramp. He docks the boat and returns with his truck, backing it down the ramp. Upon approaching the dock, he sees a group of people standing by the boat and tells them to avoid buying this brand because it's a lousy boat. That's when someone says, "Are you aware there's a trailer attached to your boat?"*

The fact that you are reading this book is evidence you are going to have a better experience at the boat ramp. See you on the water!

CHAPTER 1

The Trailer Boat

 WOULDN'T IT BE GREAT IF YOU COULD SPEND ALL
your boating time actually boating? Forget the pretrip preparation.
Forget the long-distance travel. Forget the maintenance. Just beam over
to the lake and roar off into a bright blue paradise. (There actually are places that
will store your boat, maintain it, launch it, provision it, have it ready for your
arrival, and have someone waiting at the dock when you return from a day on the
water.) But for most of us, owning a boat means spending time on a variety of off-
the-water activities. The key words here are "spending time." These are the fundamentals of boating, and in the following chapters they'll be covered in some detail.

Trailer boaters are boaters first, and everything else second. So it's appropriate to begin by focusing on the love of the boater's life—the boat.

At the launch ramp, no one has a problem spotting a trailer boat. On a typical Saturday morning you see fiberglass and aluminum runabouts and fishing
boats. You see cuddy and aft-cabin cruisers. You see walkarounds, deck boats,
pontoon boats, center consoles, flats boats, johnboats, bass boats, sailboats, and
sport boats. Increasingly, you see personal watercraft being launched as well. All
are trailer boats.

In these pages, however, we're going to focus on boats no more than
twenty-six feet long and eight feet six inches wide. With a trailer, the majority of

these towing rigs generally weigh less than six thousand pounds. Boats of this size are narrow enough to be street legal without special permits (we'll discuss this later on) and light enough to be towed by the family vehicle (we'll discuss that too). These are the heart of the trailer-boat market and, as such, they are the primary focus of this book.

However, there are a few worthy exceptions. These include classic wooden boats, rubber inflatables, canoes, kayaks, and rafts, plus powerboats and sailboats that are longer, wider, and heavier than the norm. Where applicable, the needs of these special trailer boats will be addressed.

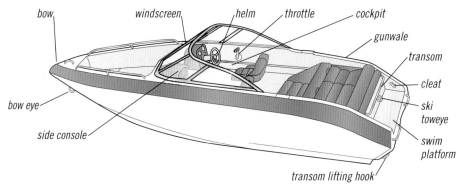

The Trailer Boat There are more than seven million trailer boats of all types and sizes registered in the U.S. The typical trailer boat is twenty-six feet long or less, eight feet six inches wide or less, and six thousand pounds or less. Maximum towing-weight ratings and highway restrictions are defining factors.

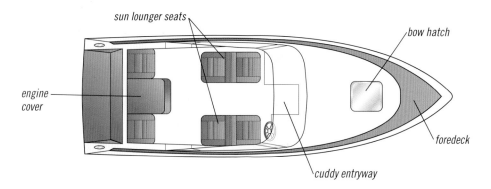

Cuddy Cabin Cuddies range from enclosed foredecks on simple runabout hulls to overnight cruisers.

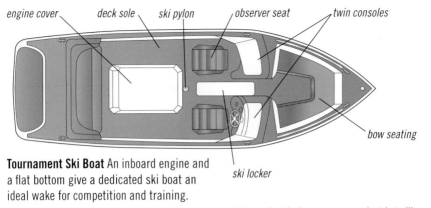

engine cover   deck sole   ski pylon   observer seat   twin consoles

bow seating

Tournament Ski Boat An inboard engine and a flat bottom give a dedicated ski boat an ideal wake for competition and training.

ski locker

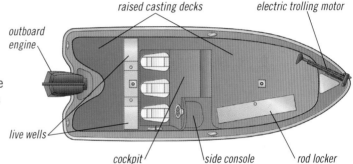

raised casting decks   electric trolling motor

outboard engine

Bass Boat Serious freshwater fishing and high performance are the twin priorities of the tournament bass boat.

live wells

cockpit   side console   rod locker

THE BASIC HULL

The component that most directly affects overall trailering and boat handling is the hull—the structural body of the boat that comes into contact with the water. It's also the part of the boat that comes in contact with the bed or cradle of the trailer.

The first things you need to know about the hull, as far as trailering is concerned, are its primary specifications: length, beam, height, and weight.

The overall length of the boat's hull, especially for trailering, is measured along the centerline from the bow to the transom. Such exterior components as the bow pulpit, swim platform, and outboard engine bracket are important for docking, storage, and performance, but don't necessarily affect the way the hull rests on the bed of the trailer. Until recently, most of these components were add-on options, but today they're often integrated into the hull's basic mold.

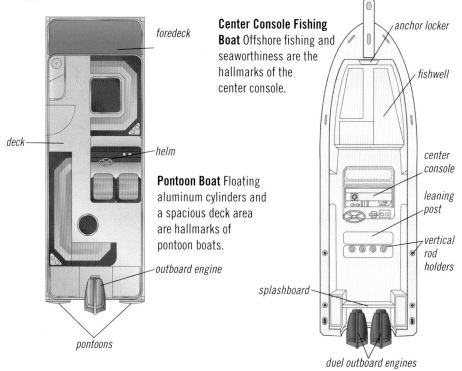

Center Console Fishing Boat Offshore fishing and seaworthiness are the hallmarks of the center console.

foredeck

anchor locker

fishwell

deck

helm

Pontoon Boat Floating aluminum cylinders and a spacious deck area are hallmarks of pontoon boats.

center console

leaning post

vertical rod holders

outboard engine

splashboard

pontoons

duel outboard engines

Unfortunately, this situation has resulted in some confusion about how overall length is listed in the manufacturer's literature. Some manufacturers include the integrated components in their measurements. Others don't. Since there is no industry standard, the best advice is to read your owner's manual carefully or go online and read the specs of your boat on the manufacturer's website to determine how the figure is obtained and what it does, or doesn't, include.

There's rarely any confusion about the boat's beam, or width. It's always measured at the hull's widest point. On federal highways and on most state and local roads, the maximum beam allowable is eight feet six inches (although some states—Georgia and Louisiana and a few others—have set eight feet as the widest a boat can be without requiring a permit). This eight-foot-six-inch limitation ensures that the vast majority of boats

On federal highways and on most state and local roads, the maximum beam allowable is eight feet six inches . . .

manufactured are narrower than this and are therefore street legal.

The figure given for weight, however, isn't so straightforward. Many manufacturers use the term "dry weight" in their literature, which technically refers to the weight of the boat before filling the fuel and freshwater tanks. Since many boaters drive on the road with empty tanks, this seems like a logical standard. Except for one thing: The term often refers to the weight of the boat prior to the installation of all the options, equipment, gear, and, most significantly, the engine. Again, the best advice is to refer to your owner's manual and the manufacturer's literature. Read them carefully.

The final specification to note is height. Although most trailer boaters rarely worry about this dimension, overhead obstructions can make for unpleasant encounters. So, after mounting your boat on the trailer, measure the distance between the ground and the bottom of the hull. Then add this dimension to the height figure listed in the factory literature. Then, make sure your VHF antennas are down. This is your trailering height.

Naturally, owners of boats with aluminum towers, flying bridges, raised helms, and fixed masts will be more concerned with trailering height than the average boater. One reassuring note is that federal highways are generally built to accommodate tractor trailers and buses up to a maximum of thirteen feet six inches. If your trailering height is a foot or more below this benchmark, you won't have much to worry about on the interstates, but it's still wise to pay careful attention to posted signs. Once you get off the superhighways, the best advice is to pay even closer attention. As a matter of fact, this is good advice to follow at all times while trailering.

HULL SHAPES

To a trailer boater, the hull's bottom shape is as important on land, where it rests on the trailer, as it is on water.

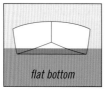

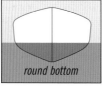

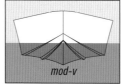

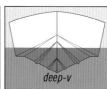

The two oldest hull designs are flat bottoms, which are found on small dinghies and rowboats, and round bottoms, which can be either full displacement or semi-displacement hulls.

Both mod-V and deep-V hulls are planing hulls that use bottom strakes to help reduce the wetted surface and improve handling.

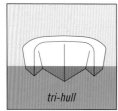

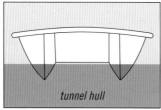

The tri-hull (or cathedral hull) is characterized by having three hull points in contact with the water. The tunnel hull rides on two points called sponsons.

Historically, trailer-boat hulls have been variations on three basic themes: flat, round, and V. Of these, the most common are V-shaped planing hulls, characterized by hard chines and the ability to lift partially out of the water at running speeds. These planing hulls fall into two categories: tri-hull (or cathedral) and classic wedge-shaped hulls.

As the name tri-hull implies, boats with this design are loosely characterized by three V-shaped side-by-side bottom components on the hull. Sometimes called cathedral hulls, they perform with efficiency and have outstanding side-to-side stability. However, they tend to pound in rough water and give a relatively wet ride. For these reasons, tri-hull boats have been phased out over the years, although many old models still ply the waterways.

Tri-hulls have been superseded in modern times by more wedgelike V hulls. These hulls are differentiated from each other by the angle of the V measured at the transom. This angle is stated in degrees of deadrise. The industry has no rigid standard to categorize V hulls, but the following classes may be used as a guide: (1) Deep-V (18° to 24°), used primarily on offshore boats; (2) Mod-V (12° to 17°), used on near-shore or saltwater or big-lake freshwater boats; (3) Flat-V (less than 12°), used primarily on lake and river boats.

The advantage of the V-hull design is its sharp entry into the water, which makes for exceptional straight-line tracking and holding tight in turns. Equally important, its sharp entry enables the boat to slice into the chop instead of pounding down hard on each wave.

Few boaters today encounter the simple but rough-riding flat hull. Exceptions are owners of johnboats, dinghies, small sailboats, and aluminum rowboats or fishing boats. Equally rare are round-bottom displacement or semidisplacement hulls. These designs are generally confined to vintage wooden boats or sailboats.

Pontoon boats and tunnel hulls are more common. Pontoon boats are characterized by twin airtight, semidisplacement hulls connected above the waterline by a platform deck. Also called catamarans, these boats are inexpensive and low powered and made with welded-aluminum pontoons. Some builders today, however, are using fiberglass pontoons that incorporate some planing characteristics to improve efficiency.

Tunnel-hull boats use the twin-hull design to achieve maximum speed. The twin hulls are designed to trap air beneath the boat and lift it out of the water for minimum drag. When the boat is running at wide-open throttle, the hulls lightly kiss the water's surface. In addition to speed, tunnel boats have terrific handling characteristics.

A typical tunnel boat has a raised center section flanked by sponsons on either side. The sponsons can be either catamaran style, which are symmetrical, or dihedral, which are half-Vs. An interesting tunnel-boat variation is the mod-VP, which has a V bottom flanked by two sponsons. This design offers the best of both worlds—riding comfort and air entrapment.

BASIC POWER

Like the hull shape, the boat's power source is as important on land as it is in the water. Each type of marine power, either engine-driven or wind-driven, affects how a boat rests on the bed of a trailer.

The most common type of power found in boating is supplied by an outboard motor, which is bolted onto the back of the boat's transom (there are approximately nine million outboard engines in America). These power plants are typically internal-combustion two-stroke or four-stroke, although technology is beginning to favor the latter. In 1992, the average outboard

Two piston strokes (up and down) are required to complete the engine's combustion cycle.

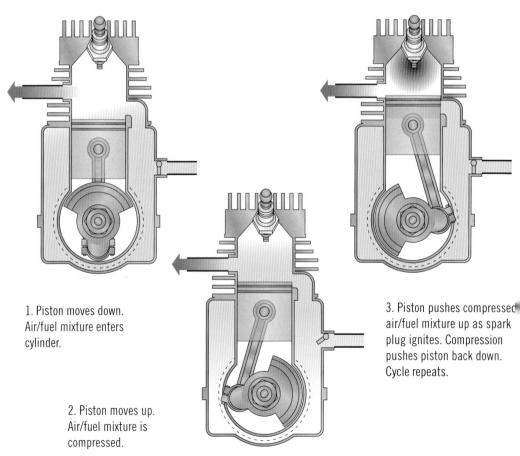

1. Piston moves down. Air/fuel mixture enters cylinder.

2. Piston moves up. Air/fuel mixture is compressed.

3. Piston pushes compressed air/fuel mixture up as spark plug ignites. Compression pushes piston back down. Cycle repeats.

Four piston strokes are required to complete the engine's combustion cycle.

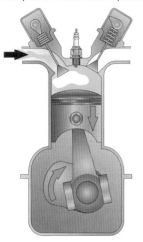

1. Piston is pulled down. Fuel/air is drawn into chamber. Intake valve closes when piston reaches bottom of downward stroke.

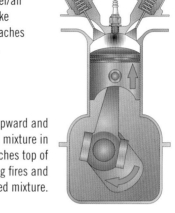

2. Piston moves upward and compresses air/fuel mixture in cylinder. As piston reaches top of cylinder, a spark plug fires and ignites the compressed mixture.

3. Mixture burns rapidly and combustion forces piston downward. This is the only stroke where power is created in a four-stroke engine.

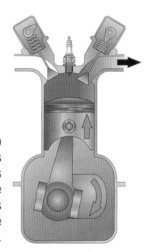

4. The piston starts moving up again now that power stroke is complete. Exhaust valve opens and hot burned gases are released. When piston reaches top of cylinder, exhaust valve closes. Cycle repeats.

engine produced 66.6 horsepower. Ten years later, the average jumped to 85.7 horsepower. This engine has become not only more powerful, but more fuel-efficient and less polluting of both air and water. This is a pivotal time for outboard motor manufacturers, as each must comply with a 2006 deadline for a 75% reduction of hydrocarbon emissions (called "the Final Rule"). They've been successful; some were compliant years ahead of the date.

But the move toward cleaner outboards hasn't doomed production of two-stroke engines. Direct fuel injection or a variation on that theme (electronic fuel injection and programmed fuel injection) are new technologies being used in two-stroke outboards to make them both cleaner burning and fuel-efficient. A few years ago, many agreed that while a four-stroke outboard was bulkier and heavier than a two-stroke, it ran cleaner and quieter. Now, both technologies are providing outboards that produce a more powerful "hole shot"—how fast the boat can go from sitting in the water to getting up on plane, while also becoming less labor intensive. Traditional two-stroke outboards required you to mix oil with gasoline (usually at a ratio of 100:1 or 50:1) to operate while the newer four-stroke outboards will do this automatically. But now, some newer two-stroke engines operate without pre-mixed oil and gas.

Outboards now range in size from a two horesepower with the fuel tank at the top of the engine to more than 300 horsepower with double fuel tanks on either side near the transom. The trend being seen in many new trailer boats is the use of double and in some instances, triple, engines mounted on a boat's transom.

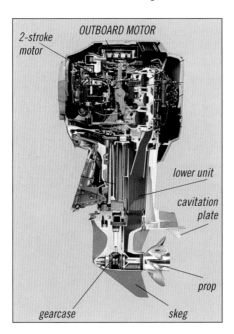

While two-stroke outboards have dominated the market for years, four-stroke engine sales now account for more than half of all new outboards sold.

But whatever the number of outboards on your boat, almost all engines are adjustable with power trim and steering systems. Trim is a term that refers to the running attitude of the boat as it's affected by the position of the motor's drive unit. On outboards equipped with power trim, the engine can be raised or lowered by pressing a control button on the throttle or steering wheel (and many trailer boaters will put this to use as soon as the boat is off the trailer).

Inboard engines are located inside the hull of the boat (hence the name) and are positioned amidships or somewhat aft. They are typically four-stroke motors that consist of automotive engine blocks that have been marinized—fixed with components and systems, such as raw-water cooling systems and flame arrestors, that enable them to cope with the harsh marine environment.

A second type of inboard engine is the diesel, which comes from the automotive world as well. Diesels are four-cycle internal combustion engines that generate tremendous compression to ignite small quantities of low-combustion diesel fuel. Compared to gas engines, diesels are very fuel-efficient, long-lived, and inexpensive to maintain. However, they're also relatively pricey and heavy. For this reason, diesels are more commonly found in yachts and larger boats.

An inboard engine runs a drive shaft through the bottom of the hull in two different ways: direct drive, which calls for the engine to be tilted on its mountings so the shaft can run in a straight line through the bottom of the

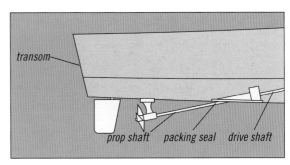

In a direct-drive configuration, an inboard system is basically a marinized automotive engine with a drive shaft that runs through the hull.

hull; and V-drive, which splits the forward facing shaft to form a V-angle before running the prop shaft back through the hull. Unlike outboards, the prop shafts on inboard engines cannot tilt out of the way during trailering.

And then there is the inboard/outboard (I/O), also known as a stern-drive engine, which has features common to both inboard and outboard

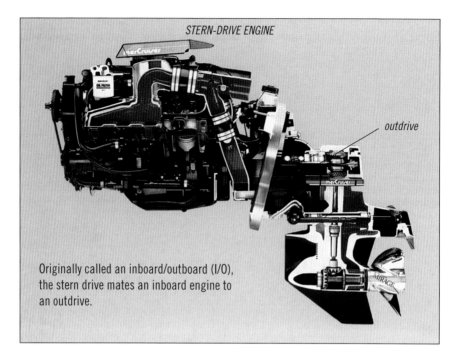

STERN-DRIVE ENGINE

outdrive

Originally called an inboard/outboard (I/O), the stern drive mates an inboard engine to an outdrive.

engines. The typical stern drive has a four-cycle, marinized automotive engine mounted just forward of the transom. The vast majority use gasoline engines. However, there are a few diesel stern drives on U.S. waterways, although they're more popular internationally.

What makes a stern drive interesting is that, instead of running the drive shaft at an angle through the bottom of the hull, it runs the shaft horizontally through a cutout in the transom. Here the shaft connects to an outdrive unit that runs vertically down into the water. It's a complicated piece of engineering that requires splitting the drive shaft twice to form a Z-shape. After the outboard, the stern drive is the second most common engine in trailer boating. Modern stern drives are equipped with power trim, and their lower units can be tilted out of the way during trailering…and during launching or retrieving.

> After the outboard, the stern drive is the second most common engine in trailer boating.

Engines on trailered sailboats will have an

effect as well. While the mast must be unhinged and dropped and the keel or centerboard well must be adaptable to the trailer, the boat's power component can be carried in the tow vehicle if it's an outboard. If it's an inboard, the engine must be considered when finding a suitable boat ramp for launching and retrieving. In order to accommodate these needs, many sailboaters use trailers with an elongated tongue so the trailer can extend farther into the water while the tow vehicle's wheels remain relatively dry. In some cases, the boat can only be moved using a tall cradle. In these instances, a boater may start thinking about renting a slip, which will be much less labor intensive for getting on the water. Now, that said, any boat can be trailered as long as the hull and the trailer are the right fit.

Except for dealing with the mast, launching and retrieving a sailboat is identical to doing the same for a powerboat. But always check carefully for overhead power lines when using a boat ramp with a sailboat.

REVIEW

1 A trailer boat can be as small as a dinghy and as large as a 50-plus-foot cigarette boat. This book concentrates on trailer boats no longer than 26 feet. Still, almost any boat can be trailered as long as the trailer is designed to fit the hull.

2 Modern trailer boat hull designs include cuddy cabin, walkaround, pontoon boat (catamaran), center cockpit, and johnboat.

3 Trailer boat specifications may vary from manufacturer to manufacturer. It's important to know the following four things: overall length, dry weight, beam, and height.

4 Most trailer boats are built with a beam (width) of eight feet six inches. Anything more than this will require a "wide load" permit for each state through which you are traveling. Know your state's requirements for trailering before buying the boat.

5 Trailer boat hull shapes can be flat bottom, round, or deep or moderate V hulls.

6 Outboards are the most common power source. Because of a pending EPA deadline, new outboard engines have to produce 75% less hydrocarbon emissions than before. Most engine manufacturers have been able to meet this deadline ahead of time. Today, there are two-stroke and four-stroke engines.

7 Inboard engines are less common, although many boat models use an inboard/outboard (I/O) stern-drive configuration that allows the engine to be raised or lowered for trim or for launching and retrieval at the boat ramp.

8 Trailering an outboard is usually done with the engine raised so the skeg and/or prop do(es)n't bottom out when going over bumps. In some cases, a transom saver is used for this purpose.

CHAPTER 2

The Trailer

 BOAT TRAILERS HAVE ALWAYS BEEN A SECONDARY purchase. The boat is selected, the tow vehicle is already owned, and only then is any thought given to the need for a boat trailer. It's difficult to get excited about them.

But having a good trailer is essential to having a successful trip to—and from—the boat ramp. So let's spend some time taking a look at the third part of the truck-boat-trailer trio.

Today, many boat dealers sell a "package," which is a particular model of boat and a trailer that is fitted for the boat's hull. The required specifications in matching a trailer and a boat include (1) the hull length, (2) the bow eye to transom length, (3) the chine beam width, and (4) the weight of the boat, including motor, batteries, fuel, and equipment. However, if you are about to purchase a boat trailer separately from the boat, it's important to understand that no single clearinghouse exists for boat trailer builders and boat manufacturers with specific hull specs. As a result, each trailer manufacturer obtains the necessary information from the boat builder individually. Usually, this works fine but every potential boat trailer owner should understand that any given trailer on a showroom floor doesn't automatically conform to the boat that you've selected. Some trailer manufacturers provide models that will work with your boat on their websites. Check with the boat or trailer manufacturer about the trailer model you have in mind (the trailer salesman should do this routinely, but if there is any question, the boat or trailer manufacturer will be able to provide advice on compatibility).

TYPES OF TRAILERS

A trailer, by definition, is a load-bearing vehicle that enables a boat to be towed by a car or truck (or an SUV). It typically consists of either an all-steel tube frame that's painted (for freshwater use) or galvanized (for salt-water use). Today, more and more boat trailers are being made of aluminum. It's more expensive than galvanized steel but it's also lighter. This means less weight to pull and that translates into better gas mileage. With the popularity of SUVs that may not have the tow capacity of many light trucks, the lighter aluminum trailer is preferable. Aluminum is also corrosion resistant so it isn't going to rust, unlike its steel counterpart. But even aluminum trailer manufacturers suggest you are better off with a steel

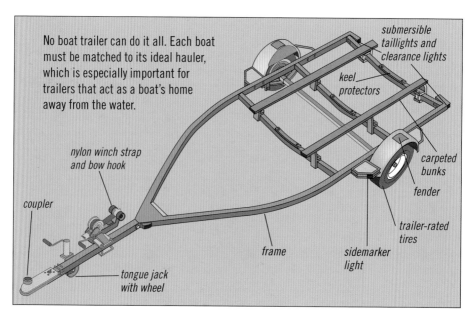

No boat trailer can do it all. Each boat must be matched to its ideal hauler, which is especially important for trailers that act as a boat's home away from the water.

submersible taillights and clearance lights

keel protectors

nylon winch strap and bow hook

coupler

carpeted bunks

fender

trailer-rated tires

frame

sidemarker light

tongue jack with wheel

trailer if your boat weight exceeds 8,500 pounds.

There are three types of common trailer designs used in boating: (1) the bunk trailer; (2) the roller trailer; and (3) the flatbed trailer.

The simple bunk trailer is the most common trailer in boating. It's suitable for a wide range of hulls, but especially boats using deep water ramps. The adjustable bunks, which are located at contact points and form the trailer cradle, are carpeted for cushioning and generally made of wood.

If possible, look for a bunk trailer that uses cypress rather than pine. Cypress is a heavy, dense wood, while pine has the capability of floating because it is so much lighter.

Bunks perform several important functions: First, they position the boat so that it balances properly over the axle. Second, they hold the boat securely in place by lining up the hull points that are internally supported (this is an important spec provided by the boat manufacturer and used by the trailer manufacturer when designing the appropriate trailer for use with a particular hull). Third, they spread out the points of stress to prevent potential hull deformities, which can result from poor alignment.

Roller trailers use rubber or plastic rollers in place of bunks. The

Versatile bunk trailers are used for small personal watercraft (PWC) as well as big cruisers.

rollers are usually mounted on adjustable or fixed brackets. The result is the smoothest and easiest method of moving the boat on and off the trailer. Roller trailers are especially well suited for shallow-water ramps.

Compared to bunk trailers, roller trailers are equipped with extra hardware—often a dozen or more roller assemblies and a handful of brackets. These add cost and require increased maintenance (replacing broken or cracked rollers is a common repair). Many boaters believe the benefits of law-friction launching and retrieval outweigh the disadvantages; however, the advent of modern, well-designed drive-on bunk trailers has greatly reduced the need for rollers. Still, the choice of rollers or bunks is similar to that of a Mac or a PC. Everyone has a preference.

Bunk and roller trailers aren't mutually exclusive. Many trailers combine the best of both. Keel rollers, for example, are commonly found on bunk trailers, especially for midsize and large boats. The keel rollers help ease the boat on and off the trailer, and provide support at a pivotal point in the cradle. Conversely, keel pads, rear bunk assemblies, and forward bunk

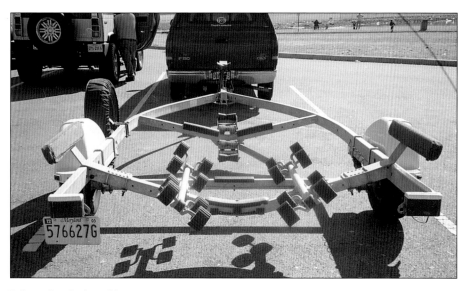

Rollers allow for launching ease.

pads appear on roller trailers. The additional bunks help capture the boat during retrieval and improve hull support while on the road.

To the typical boater, the flatbed trailer refers to a relatively small trailer with a simple bed made of planks or plywood. These carryall workhorses have many uses, but they're generally limited to light specialized craft. Although flatbeds can be equipped with fixed or temporary cradles to hold large V-bottom, semidisplacement, or deep-keel boats, rigs like these require a hoist for launching and therefore see infrequent service by the vast majority of trailer boaters.

The beauty of the flatbed design is that it's so simple and versatile that it works as well in the tractor-trailer class for large yachts as it does for owners of personal watercraft, flat-bottom aluminum boats, pontoon boats, canoes, kayaks, and inflatables.

A flatbed also works well for the boater who wants to use it for double duty: annual boat launching and retrieving (through the use of a removable cradle), plus utility work. For these boaters, it should be noted that bunk trailers can be converted for double duty too. The conversion from a bunk to a flatbed involves removing the bunk brackets and then bolting down a sturdy wooden frame and bed.

Without bunks or rollers to hold a boat in place, flatbeds are commonly equipped with guide bars, tie downs, support racks, and other add-on accessories. One feature that's sometimes used on small flatbed trailers is a hinged tongue or hinged frame, which enables the bed to tilt like a dump truck. Although tilt-bed trailers aren't recommended for craft of substantial size or weight, they're used for boats small enough to be muscled around during launching and retrieval.

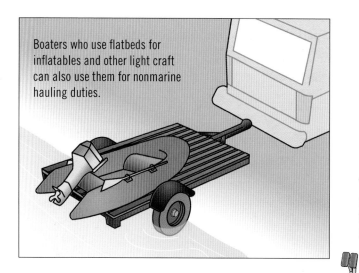

Boaters who use flatbeds for inflatables and other light craft can also use them for nonmarine hauling duties.

The long bunks of the pontoon boat trailer require tandem axles to improve road handling.

TRAILER TIRES

Trailer boaters might take a look from time to time at the tires on their trailer prior to going out on the road. To quote Martha Stewart, "it's a good thing" (although chances are good she wasn't talking about boat trailer tires). Inflation and tire wear on a boat trailer are no different from inflation and tire wear on your tow vehicle or passenger car. Both need to be inspected. To put this in per-

. . . tire troubles have accounted for 43% of all calls to the BoatU.S. Dispatch Center over the past three years from trailer boaters who found themselves stranded on the side of the highway. . .

spective; tire troubles have accounted for 43% of all calls to the BoatU.S.

Dispatch Center over the past three years from trailer boaters who found themselves stranded on the side of the highway (it's part of the Trailer Assist Tow Program that is available to members).

The first step in getting to know your tire is to take a look at the writing on the sidewall. Everything you need to know is found right here. Let's pick a tire and see what it tells us:

A typical trailer tire has size, maximum PSI, and type (radial or bias ply) listed on the sidewall.

▶ ST or not ST?

Tires that are designed for trailers (boat-horse-utility) always have the designation of ST (special trailer), although there are some manufacturers that identify their tires with the words "for trailer use only." If you see a P, the tire is designed for a passenger car and if the tire has LT on the sidewall, it's designed for a light truck. In the event you are negotiating to buy a boat trailer and the tires don't have ST, this is the moment for some negotiating. Unfortunately, there are many stories of brand-new trailers being sold without ST tires so be sure to spend some time with the sidewall before making a deal. Trailer tires have stronger sidewalls in order to support the weight of the boat when going around corners. If you are using tires that aren't ST, it is possible your insurance company will refuse to settle a claim in the event of an accident. That's how important the ST is on your tire.

▶ **215** This is the measurement (in millimeters) of the tire width. In this example, the tire is 215 mm wide (the width varies depending on the weight the tire is designed to carry). Some other common widths are 175, 185, 205, 225, and 235. The bigger this number, the wider the tire.

▶ **75** This is the aspect ratio, a fancy term for the tire's sidewall height as compared to the tire's width (in this example the height is 75% of the width). Aspect ratio on boat trailer tires is usually 75 or 80.

▶ **R or Bias Ply** Tires are either radials or bias ply. Marking a bias ply isn't standardized as it is with marking a radial with an R. If it has an R, you know it's radial. If it doesn't, it's a bias ply. If the load range is included in the sidewall specs, it is usually added after the wheel size (see item below). Radials are used for long-range trips while bias ply are more common for use on short jaunts to the local boat ramp. Bias ply are less expensive.

▶ **14** This means the tire is mounted on a 14-inch wheel. Boat trailer wheels range in size from 8-inch (for light jon boats) to 15inches for heavier cruisers and sailboats.

When you consider boat trailer tires, give serious thought as well to carrying a spare tire. Strange as it may seem, while a car manufacturer always includes a spare tire and jack in the trunk, very rarely is this done by trailer manufacturers. This keeps the price down, but when you have a flat and no spare, you may lose sight of the savings. Pay the extra money and have a spare tire mounted on the trailer. And carry a jack designed for use on the trailer (there are too many stories of tow vehicle jacks not fitting boat trailers. It's worth the extra cost).

TIRE FACTS

• Check the PSI of your tire *before* going out on the road. Maximum inflation should be done when the tire is cold (as the tire goes down the road, heat is generated and air expands). If you add air after an hour of interstate travel, be careful. The additional air will expand, possibly beyond the maximum PSI.

• Some boaters deflate their tires as a way to get their boat and trailer up (or down) a steep or slick ramp. This is a common practice and there is nothing wrong with it. Just be careful to reinflate the tires prior to going back on the road or you may be in for a memorable ride back home.

• Know the load range of your trailer tires (A,B,C,D,E). A is the lightest in the range—E is the heaviest. As the load range increases, so too will the required PSI. If you are pulling a boat and trailer and fuel and water and equipment, then that's the load range of the tire you are going to need. Don't buy tires based on "dry weight" of the boat alone—that doesn't include the weight of fuel (about 6 pounds/gallon) and water (about 8.33 pounds/gallon).

• Just because a tire store sells tires for cars, trucks, and SUVs doesn't mean it sells tires for boat trailers. Marine stores will usually have tires with ST on the sidewall.

WHEEL BEARINGS

The components designed to allow the tires and wheels to roll freely are the wheel bearings, which are two rings of steel rollers located inside the wheel hubs. The wheel bearings rotate around a part of the axle called the spindle. For the bearings to work properly, the hubs need to be well packed with grease.

Just as there are bunk trailers and roller trailers, there are advocates of lithium-complex grease and calcium-based grease to lubricate bearings. Lithium-complex grease is designed for temperatures as high as 325 degrees and has high water resistance. Calcium-based grease is standard with many new boat trailer manufacturers and has been around longer than the lithium products. Don't mix these greases: use either one or the other in the hub.

But whatever grease is used, be sure it says "marine grade" on the tube. Bearings don't like water, and grease that is designed for water (i.e., marine grade) provides the very best protection. If you notice the bearing grease in your hubs is milky colored, this is an indication of water being present. To put it another way: it's time to change the bearing grease. There is no hard rule as to how often the bearing grease should be changed because it depends on how often the boat trailer is used. A general rule is to change grease every 3,000 miles. If you trailer less than this in a year, be sure to inspect the grease as often as possible.

A newer bearing system uses oil rather than grease to lubricate the bearings (oil bath). It has been a standard part of semi trailer hubs for years and has been introduced only recently in boat trailers. These new hubs have an oil level indicator cap that can be easily and quickly read to determine if the bearings are adequately protected.

Bearings have three ways of telling you there's trouble ahead; the trick is knowing what to look for and maybe more importantly, when to look for it. (1) If you jack your trailer wheel up enough so that it can spin freely, the wheel should spin quietly. If you hear a noise, that is reason for concern about the bearings. If you hear the noise while under way, pull over as quickly as possible. (2) If grease can be seen on the boat hull near where it sits above the tire, that's a clear indication that a seal has begun to leak. (3) If the hub feels hot when you pull into a gas station, rest stop, or restaurant, that's an early warning that the bearings are failing.

grease piston fitting *outer bearing* *inner bearing* *axle* *rear seal* *bearing protector* *spring* *wheel hub* *spindle* *bearing race* *dust cap*

Sooner or later all boat trailers submerge their wheels, which means they should be equipped with bearing protectors to keep the wheel bearings packed with lubricant.

AXLES

Here's an "axle rule" for boats and boat trailers: If your boat is less than 20 feet long, a single axle boat trailer will probably accommodate your needs. If the boat is between 20–30 feet, you are going to need a double axle trailer. If it is longer than 30 feet, a triple axle trailer is the ticket. Another way to look at the axle rule is this: the heavier the boat being pulled, the more its weight needs to be distributed on the trailer. By distributing the boat's weight over two axles and suspension systems, a trailer is able to achieve improved on-road smoothness and stability, reduced tendency to sway from side to side, decreased sensitivity to improper tongue weight, and an increased margin of safety in the event of a flat tire. To help accomplish this, a good tandem-axle trailer will be equipped with load equalizer bars that distribute the shock loads between the adjoining suspension systems and minimize the impact.

The heavier the boat being pulled, the more its weight needs to be distributed on the trailer.

Many trailer manufacturers use designs allowing the axle(s) to be moved on the trailer frame. This feature allows the boater to position the boat on the trailer better so that the load is balanced. If tongue weight is too high on the tow vehicle hitch, moving the trailer's axle forward can correct the problem.

BRAKES

One of the biggest changes in boat trailer design in the past decade concerns brake systems. There are more designs from which to choose but the greater challenge is keeping current with state regulations regarding brakes on boat trailers. Each state has its own rules about when brakes are required so it is important for every new boat trailer owner to know the rules before walking into a marine store to buy a trailer. Unfortunately, too many salesmen out there are eager to say "it's not a problem" or "it's legal" when the facts are otherwise. In general, brakes are required on boat trailers that carry anywhere from 1,000 pounds (Gross Vehicle Weight Rating or GVWR— weight of the trailer fully loaded) in North Carolina to 5,000 pounds (GVWR) in Alaska. Most states require brakes on a trailer carrying more than 3,000 pounds; just a few states have no brake requirement whatsoever (North Dakota, Missouri). Some states, such as Florida—which requires brakes on all boat trailers carrying 3,000 pounds or more—require brakes on all axles of the trailer. Bottom line: the National Association of State Boating Law Administrators website has all the information you'll need for every state (www.nasbla.org/blas/htm).

There are two common braking systems currently in use on boat trailers, surge and electric, with surge being the more common. Surge brakes work by sensing a sudden slowing of forward momentum (or sometimes by the dipping of the tow vehicle's rear bumper when braking takes place, or sometimes both). When the tow vehicle brakes are applied, the forward motion of the trailer pushes it into a coupler at the trailer hitch; this in turn activates a piston rod in the master cylinder, triggering the trailer brakes. As a result, the harder the brakes are applied in the tow vehicle, the harder the brakes are applied on the trailer.

Of course, if the brakes work only when the trailer is pushing toward the tow vehicle, this would seem to defy a boater backing a trailer down the boat ramp. If properly attached, a solenoid will activate when the tow vehicle is placed in reverse (it works when the backup lights are on), thus allowing the brakes to take hold as the trailer goes down the ramp. Some boaters have to readjust the solenoid manually on the actuator before backing down the ramp and then remember to reset it in order to go up the ramp and back on the road.

In the event the trailer becomes separated from the tow vehicle, a "breakaway" system is set into motion. It is a short cable running from the receiver hitch on the tow vehicle to the master cylinder on the boat trailer. If the trailer becomes loose, the cable pulls on the master cylinder and the brakes are applied.

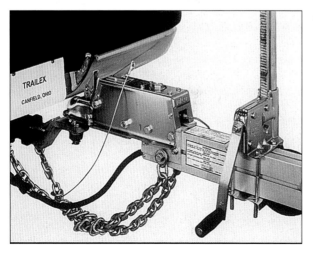

A sudden slowing of forward momentum activates the hydraulic surge brake.

The second brake system gaining popularity on boat trailers is electric. While the idea of anything electric being used anywhere near water isn't appealing, electric brakes are appearing more and more on new trailers. Recreational vehicles and horse trailers have used electric brakes for years and now, with improved technology, boat trailers have adopted the system. The connections are securely encased in resin and users report quicker braking action (unlike surge brakes, electric brakes don't rely on a forward push from the trailer before activating) and increased sensitivity. If you decide to use electric brakes, trailer experts suggest installing a freshwater flushkit that connects to a garden hose to clean out the brakes after being submerged during launch and retrieval.

There are two methods used in brake systems, drum and disc. Drum brakes have more moving parts but remain the most popular, although new boat trailers are being made with disc brakes. When servicing drum brakes, changing the brake shoes is just part of the job. Insist that all the springs and fittings also be replaced. Every time the brake pedal is depressed, a piston pushes against the brake shoe, which in turn presses it against the brake drum. The boat trailer slows down.

Disc brakes can be compared to the center pull style brakes on a bicycle. Changing brake pads is the most common maintenance required and they'll let you know it's due by the squeals they emit whenever you apply the brake pedal. While this is always a good way to know it's time to have the brakes serviced, remember that the trailer is behind the tow vehicle: you may not hear the squeal if the windows are up and the radio is playing. Disc brake rotors are the other major maintenance job and, when worn, you'll feel a shudder or vibration whenever you apply the brakes.

So, which to use? Disc brakes are more expensive. Drum brakes have a track record. Both operate in water, which means whatever system you have, make sure you have it serviced before going on the road.

SUSPENSION SYSTEMS

To avoid punishing metal-to-metal connections (read: to make the ride smoother), trailer frames are suspended from their axles one of three different ways: leaf springs, coil springs, or torsion bars. Of the three, leaf springs are the most used but torsion-bar suspension is getting more common with every new line of boat trailers.

Like wheel bearing protectors and surge brakes, leaf springs are mechanically simple. The axle is suspended below the frame by resting on leaves, or strips of steel, which flex when the wheels go over a bump. The leaves are connected to the frame by hangers and shackles. Light boats like canoes, inflatables, kayaks, and single-man sailboats may only need a single leaf spring on a boat trailer, while larger boats may use seven or more.

For light loads, a single steel leaf can provide adequate suspension. Heavier loads require multiple steel leaves.

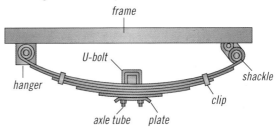

Coil springs, often employed in conjunction with shock absorbers in a system called coil-over shocks, are far more common in cars and trucks than they are on boat trailers. You aren't going to find them very often on a boat trailer built in the past ten years, but if you do, keep in mind they are vulnerable to corrosion.

Torsion-bar systems have these benefits: the center of gravity is lowered on the trailer because the height of the trailer is reduced with torsion bars, installation is easy; and there is independent suspension among the wheels, which means road bumps are better absorbed. Disadvantages are that they are more costly than leaf springs and, if water does get inside, there is a risk of corrosion. If a torsion system is damaged, it is non-repairable and will have to be replaced. Something else to think about is where you are going to be trailering your boat. If you are in a remote area and something happens to your torsion bar, replacement will take longer and be costlier than repairing a leaf spring.

Essentially, this maintenance-free, independently acting system consists of a hexagonal exterior axle made of tubular steel that encloses a three-sided solid steel shaft. The solid shaft in turn is surrounded by three (or four) rubber inserts. At the ends of the axle, the wheels are mounted on hubs connected to spindles, which extend from the solid inner shaft. Since there are no metal-to-metal moving parts, a torsion system is going to operate more quietly than a leaf spring system.

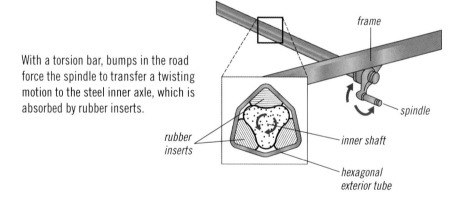

With a torsion bar, bumps in the road force the spindle to transfer a twisting motion to the steel inner axle, which is absorbed by rubber inserts.

frame

rubber inserts

spindle

inner shaft

hexagonal exterior tube

LIGHTS

Both sides of the rear of the trailer are required to have combination reflector-type lights that act as stoplights (red), taillights (red), turn signals (amber or red), and side markers (red). Another light is required for the license plate (white), and both sides of the trailer must have side-marker lights (red in the rear and amber in front). Side and rear reflectors are also required. Some boats will carry a light on the transom or outboard so that anyone following closely behind can see when brakes are applied and take appropriate action.

Trailers wider than eighty inches have several additional requirements: A tight cluster of three identification lamps (red) along the center line on the rear; four clearance lamps with two on either side of the front (amber) and either side of the rear (red); and the stop lamps and turn signals must not be less than twelve square inches in area. Regardless of size, taillights must be set a minimum of fifteen inches above the ground and a maximum of seventy-two inches high for stop lamps and eighty-three inches high for turn signal lamps. Trailers greater than thirty feet in length, less than six feet in length, or less than thirty inches wide have fewer requirements.

Trailer lights are powered and activated by the tow vehicle's electrical system, which is connected to the trailer by means of a plug with prongs that number four, five, six, or even seven. Although there are exceptions, a color-coded wiring scheme is standard: brown wire for taillights, rear marker lights, side marker lights, and license light; yellow wire for left stop and turn lights; green wire for right stop and turn lights; and white wire for the ground.

LED (Light Emitting Diode) lights are receiving rave reviews from trailer boat owners across the country. With a life as much as six times longer than standard incandescent lights, LED technology is here to stay (the standard incandescent boat trailer bulb will burn about 15,000 hours. LEDs burn 100,000 hours). Most road repair crews working at night, airport runways, and cross country semi trucks are using LED lights. There is no filament in the bulb; instead, there is a chemical bead that lights up when electricity is applied. Because it's a chemical rather than a filament, the LED burns cooler and there's no filament to break. This is good news for the anxious trailer boat owner who doesn't have to be concerned about blowing a bulb when the trailer backs into the water. And then there is the responsiveness of these new lights. While there is a lag before incandescent brake lights go on when the brakes are applied, LED lights respond two-tenths of a second faster. That fraction of a second can be the difference between a close call and an accident.

FORWARD COMPONENTS

The forward part of the trailer is called the tongue and it includes several important components. These are the winch, the winch stand, the bow stop, the bow eye safety chain, and the tongue jack. Several other components associated with the coupler will be covered in chapter 3.

The tongue itself can have several configurations. The hinged tongue on

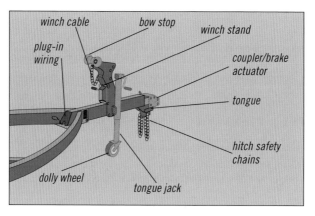

The tongue end of a trailer consists of components that secure the boat to the trailer and the trailer to the hitch.

a tilt-bed trailer is one example already covered. Two others are removable tongues and extension tongues. Each has its own purpose, the former relating to secure storage and the latter to convenient launching.

The removable tongue allows a boater to fit a trailer into a space where length may be a problem, and provides a measure of security against theft. Without a tongue, a trailer is difficult to steal. Extension tongues enable a trailer to back farther into the water without submerging the tow vehicle. Deep keel boats and shallow launch ramps (especially in areas where drought is a concern) may require the use of tongue extensions. Some trailers have a third tongue feature, a swing-away hinge that has space-saving value for storage (helping to fit a 24-foot-long boat and trailer into a 23-foot-long garage). Tongues with swing-away hinges are usually not a standard part of a boat trailer and are available only as optional equipment.

The strong pulling power of a winch is used primarily to help control the boat during retrieval and launching. It also enables a boater to snug a boat to the bow stop on the winch stand and solidly hold it in place for on-road support and security.

There are two kinds of common winches: manual hand crank (one-speed and two-speed) and electric. The electric winch is the ultimate in no-effort retrieval, but most owners of small and mid-size boats get by with mechanically simple (and affordable) manual winches. For large boats, two-speed manual or electric winches are recommended. Electric winches are connected to the tow vehicle's battery by a special wiring harness.

For the winch to work properly, it should be mounted at the same height as the boat's bow eye or above it. The connection between the winch and the bow eye is handled by a steel hook and a length of woven synthetic strap or steel cable. The length of the strap or cable should be significantly greater than the length of the boat.

Although the winch stand or post is fixed firmly in place during use, its position is adjustable. Ideally, it should be placed so that the transom rests directly over supporting bunks or rollers. Bolted in place, the winch stand acts as an anchor for the boat during all phases of trailering.

To cushion the boat/trailer connection against the winch stand, rubber blocks or stops are used. This is called a bow stop. A short safety chain hangs on the bow stop and hooks to the bow eye. The chain acts as an emergency backup in case the winch line loosens or breaks.

The final component associated with the tongue is a jack. The tongue jack enables the boater to raise and lower the tongue (usually performed when placing the trailer tongue on or removing it from the tow vehicle hitch). There are two types of tongue jacks: a drop-through jack, which simply moves up and down, and often has a removable dolly wheel or steel foot; and a swivel jack, which pivots out of the way when not in use.

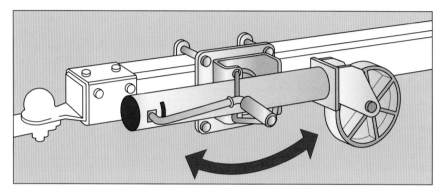

Dolly-Style Tongue Jack Using a dolly-style tongue jack is like having an extra peerson helping to move the trailer manually. It swings down to support the tongue, or up for traveling on the road. Some models remain vertical and are cranked up or down.

REVIEW

Consider these ten points when matching your boat to a trailer.

1 If your boating is done exclusively in fresh water, a painted finish is all you need. But if a part of your boating is done in salt water, even a small part, a trailer with a galvanized finish is recommended. Aluminum trailers won't corrode in either fresh water or salt water.

2 Bunk-type and roller-type trailers can be adapted to any kind of hull configuration, although rollers are unnecessary for boats that require a hoist for launching and retrieval. If you often launch at ramps under conditions that make powering on difficult, then roller-type trailers will provide an advantage. If you launch at a ramp with a gradual incline, a bunk trailer will work just fine. If you are unsure, visit the boat ramp(s) you intend to use most often and see what other boaters are using.

3 Keep in mind that it's important for the hull to be well-supported along the chines, at the transom (especially for outboard-powered boats), along the keel, and at other points where there's internal structural support. The more points of contact there are between the boat and the trailer, the better. This will spread out stress and help avoid hull deformities.

4 If your trailer will be used as a dry dock for significant periods of time, bunk trailers have an edge because of their long points of contact. Roller-type trailers will work so long as the rollers are large and numerous.

5 Flatbed trailers can be adapted to any kind of hull, but they will require cradles or racks for anything other than flat-bottom boats.

6 If your boat is light enough to be muscled around—for example, an aluminum johnboat—a tilt-bed trailer can be effective. However, most boats are too heavy for this.

7 Trailers less than 80 inches wide are ideal for small and medium size boats up to roughly 2,000 pounds. Wider trailers, up to 102 inches wide (eight and a half feet), can handle loads beyond 10,000 pounds. Wide trailers are more stable on the road than narrow ones, and they're also more costly. It is important to note that the maximum boat trailer width in most states is 102 inches (Virginia, New Jersey, and Pennsylvania have maximum widths of eight feet. Hawaii is nine feet). If your trailer—or boat that sits on the trailer—exceeds that maximum width, you are required to obtain a wide load permit for each state through which you are traveling.

8 To calculate the carrying capacity you need for your trailer, start with the dry weight of your boat and then add up all the extras. This will include the engine (if not included in the dry weight), anchor and chain, lines, fenders, batteries, Coast Guard-required safety equipment, water skis, tubes, fishing gear, spare parts, fuel (6.2 lbs/gallon), water (8.3 lbs/gallon), and a full ice chest stocked with food and beverages. Then, add 20% just to be safe (even if this means moving up to the next size trailer). This final number will be the capacity your trailer needs to be able to carry.

9 In general, most boats that are less than 20 feet in length can be safely towed on a single axle trailer. If longer than 20 feet, you will need to consider a tandem or triple-axle trailer.

10 A correctly balanced trailer carries most of its weight over the axle (or axles) and only a small percentage of weight (7–10% of the weight of the fully loaded boat and trailer) on the trailer tongue. Know the tongue weight and know that tongue weight can change from day to day as a result of fuel consumption. If your trailer sways from side to side while under way, you may need more tongue weight on the tow vehicle hitch.

CHAPTER 3

The Hitch

YOUR HITCH IS TO YOUR TOW VEHICLE AND your trailer (and the boat it carries) as your neck is to your head and your body: the connection is that essential. You can't move the trailer without the tow vehicle, and they're connected by the hitch.

In general, the hitch is a mechanism that connects a movable load carrier (the trailer) to a vehicle that pulls it (the tow vehicle). It is bolted to multiple points along the undercarriage of the car, SUV, or truck. The hitch is primarily a fixed ball-mount platform or receiver box and includes hooks for attaching safety chains. Of course, the most visible part of all is the hitch ball.

Several other components complete the hitch connection. These are located on the trailer tongue and include a coupler, an electric wiring harness, safety chains, and a surge brake cable. While these aren't technically part of the hitch, they're indispensable to the working link between the trailer and the tow vehicle.

HITCH CLASSIFICATIONS

Hitches, couplers, and hitch balls are all weight-bearing components and all use a maximum capacity rating system based on the GVWR (Gross Vehicle Weight Rating) of the trailer; put another way, the weight rating of the hitch is based on the combined weight of the trailer, boat, and engine. Hitches are also rated for tongue weight. As noted in Chapter 2, boaters want tongue weights that range from 7–10% of the trailer's GVWR. Tongue weight is based on the weight of the fully loaded boat and trailer on the hitch. It's the actual weight

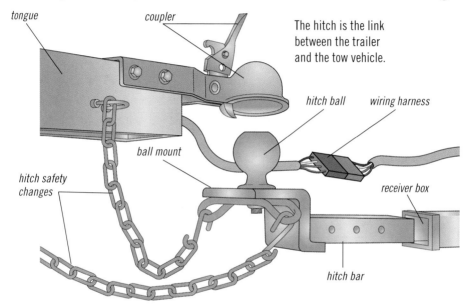

tongue

coupler

The hitch is the link between the trailer and the tow vehicle.

hitch ball   *wiring harness*

ball mount

hitch safety changes

receiver box

hitch bar

and has nothing to do with the trailer's GVWR—that only measures how much weight the trailer can handle.

Of the two weight ratings, the more important one—that of the hitch—is based on the trailer's GVWR. As a result, the hitch on your tow vehicle is in one of four classes:

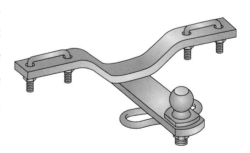

Class I This is the lightest category with a maximum capacity rating of 2,000 pounds (your boat, trailer, engine, equipment, and fuel

With a few frame attachment points, the Class I hitch is for light towing up to 2,000 pounds.

weigh no more than 2,000 pounds). The typical hitch attachment points for Class I are the bumper plus two points on the frame of the tow vehicle.

Class II This is the medium-duty category with a maximum capacity of 3,500 pounds. Typical hitch attachment points are two or more on the tow vehicle frame.

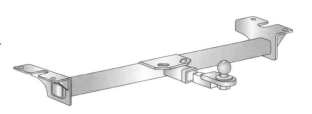

The Class II hitch is for medium towing up to 3,500 pounds. This one is shown with a removable receiver box.

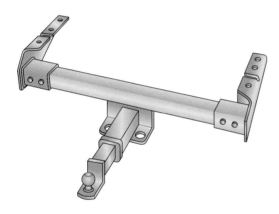

Class III This is the heavy-duty category with a maximum capacity rating of 5,000 pounds. Typical attachment points are four or more areas on the tow vehicle frame.

Class IV This is the extra heavy-duty category with a maximum capacity rating of 10,000 pounds. Typical attachment points are four or more on the tow vehicle frame.

Class III & IV Hitches
For heavy towing up to 5,000 pounds, the Class III hitch with its multiple frame attachment points is required. For heavier towing up to 10,000 pounds, a stouter Class IV hitch is required.

HITCH TYPES

In addition to the four weight-rating classes, hitches come in different styles, depending on the job to be done. Light-duty Class I hitches, for example, are offered in four types:

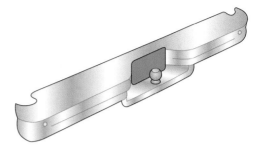

Step-bumper hitches that have attachment points on the frame can carry heavy loads. Those that don't are more for cosmetics than load carrying.

1. Frame-Mount Hitch, which is mounted solely on the frame.

2. Bumper/Frame-Mount Hitch, which is mounted to both the frame and the bumper.

3. Step Bumper, which is a rear bumper with a built-in ball-mount platform or cutaway space to install one.

4. Bumper Hitch, which is attached solely to the bumper.

Of these four styles, the frame-mount hitch is the best because it has bolted or welded attachment points on the frame. This helps distribute tongue weight off the bumper and onto the rear axle of the tow vehicle.

The bumper/frame-mount hitch can be useful for light towing, but it has a drawback: it tends to compromise the crash-resistance of the five-mph bumper, which is designed to yield slightly upon impact to absorb collision stress.

The step bumper, which is generally found on trucks, is the second-best hitch mount because it, too, relies on solid base attachment points on the frame. However, boaters should be aware that there are a number of aftermarket step bumpers that have no frame attachment points. These are useful only for the lightest of towing loads and aren't recommended for trailer boating.

Removable bumper-mount hitches are becoming more rare in towing and aren't recommended for most trailer boaters.

The final light-towing system, the bumper-mount hitch, is the least desirable. Quite simply, bumpers on cars aren't designed to handle the loads and stresses of towing. While hitches and trailers are made of steel, modern bumpers are made of a light alloy. Check your owner's manual and you'll find that both automotive and trailer manufacturers strongly advise against using bumper-mount hitches. If that isn't persuasive enough, consider the insurance company that is covering your boat: if a claim is filed because a bumper hitch breaks apart, the insurance company may refuse to pay, claiming the boat (and trailer) weren't being properly towed.

Medium and heavy towing require frame-mounted hitches, and these too come in several styles. Of the variations, two are the most common—the fixed ball-mount platform, which is a one-piece unit, and the receiver hitch, which has a removable ball-mount platform or hitch bar that slides into a receiver box.

Receiver-type hitches are by far the more versatile of the two. They enable boaters to remove hitch bars

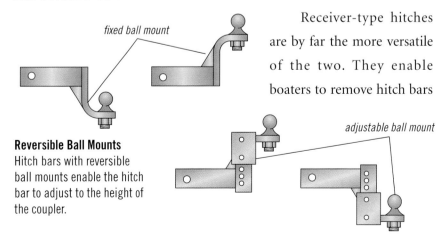

fixed ball mount

adjustable ball mount

Reversible Ball Mounts
Hitch bars with reversible ball mounts enable the hitch bar to adjust to the height of the coupler.

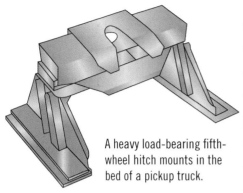

A heavy load-bearing fifth-wheel hitch mounts in the bed of a pickup truck.

and store them inside the tow vehicle when not in use. This feature not only forestalls rust, it prevents theft while enabling easy adjustment of hitch height. This can be important to boaters with multiple trailers or towing loads. The height adjustment is done through the use of extensions and reversible hitch bars.

Two other variations are fifth-wheel and weight-distributing hitches, which are generally reserved for very heavy loads. Fifth-wheel hitches are mounted in the rear bed of pickup trucks and, except for extremely large boats, they're rarely used for trailer boating.

Weight-distributing hitches are somewhat more common. These hitches spread out tongue weight through the use of spring bars so that all the tow vehicle's wheels share it. Many automotive manufacturers require the use of weight-distributing hitches, while many trailer manufacturers caution against using them; their concern is that too much stress is placed on the trailer tongue because of the trailer's wishbone design. The best advice is to read your owner's manual carefully before installing one. If properly attached and used, a weight-distributing hitch will improve both the tow vehicle's steering and braking while pulling the trailer. But if the weight of what you

Steel-spring bars on heavy-towing weight-distributing hitches distribute tongue weight to the front of the tow vehicle.

plan to tow is such an issue that you are considering a weight-distributing hitch, give some thought to getting a larger tow vehicle with greater towing capacity—that may be the safest solution of all.

HITCH BALLS

The hitch ball on the tow vehicle fits directly into the coupler on the trailer. As its name indicates, this component is basically a sphere made of solid steel. There are two-piece hitch balls on the market and while they are inexpensive, this isn't the place to start saving a few dollars. As the saying goes, you get what you pay for. Avoid them.

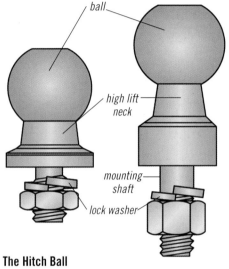

The Hitch Ball
Ball diameter and shank size affect the hitch ball's maximum load rating. Note that a high-lift neck can be used to adjust the height of the hitch ball.

The hitch ball is fixed to the end of a neck that can be either short or tall depending on the height that's best suited to the trailer. The neck, in turn, is connected to a mounting shank with a threaded end. A locking washer and a nut secure the mounting shank to a ball-mount platform or a removable hitch bar.

Hitch balls themselves come in two common diameter sizes: $1\frac{7}{8}$ inches for light towing up to 2,000 pounds (for Class I hitches) and 2 inches for loads up to 5,000 pounds (for Class II and Class III hitches). For Class IV hitches, a ball diameter of $2\frac{5}{16}$ inches is required. Shanks come in varying diameters too: $\frac{5}{8}$ inch, $\frac{3}{4}$ inch, 1 inch, and $1\frac{1}{4}$ inch. The wider the diameter, the stronger the shank and the higher the weight rating.

THE COUPLER

After the hitch ball, the coupler is the second most important contact point in the metal-to-metal connection between the trailer and the tow vehicle. Located on the very end of the trailer tongue, the coupler comes in two basic

A screw-type coupler, also known as a twist-lock coupler.

The common lever-type coupler is popular because it has a built-in safety latch. Also, it can be easily secured with a padlock.

types—the screw or hand-wheel type and the lever type. Both styles have a coupler socket that fits snugly over the hitch ball and a clamp that locks the ball in place.

The design difference between the two coupler styles is in how the ball clamp is controlled. In one, the ball clamp loosens and tightens by turning a screw knob or a hand wheel. In the other, raising or lowering a lever controls the clamp. Either style can accommodate typical trailer boat loads, but the lever type is more common. Both styles have adjustable locking nuts that alter the tension of the clamp on the ball for fine-tuning.

Lever-type couplers provide an extra margin of safety through the use of a trigger-lock mechanism, which probably accounts for their popularity. When the lever handle is pushed down to tighten the clamp, a separate safety device catches to hold the lever in the down position. This trigger lock must be released before the lever can be flipped up again to loosen the clamp.

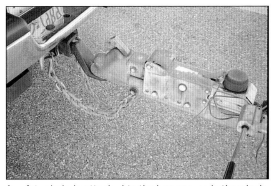

A safety chain is attached to the bow eye, as is the winch cable. Both are needed for a safe trailering trip.

SAFETY CHAINS

While the coupler incorporates a well-designed locking system, modern hitches also provide a backup mechanism for extra safety. This failsafe is two safety chains that are fitted with shackles (although most boaters use S hooks, shackles are safer). The safety chains are attached to the trailer tongue or coupler, giving added assurance that your trailer won't detach from the tow vehicle while under way. The chains are slipped through rings or holes on either side of the hitch ball. *Be sure the chains cross each other beneath the tongue.* This ensures that, if a separation does occur, the trailer tongue is caught by the chains and doesn't hit the pavement at a high speed. The chains should be

S hooks are used to attach the safety chain to the trailer, but shackles are safer.

Shackles are attached to a safety cable, which is being used more and more instead of chains.

Inspect the chains before every trip with your boat.   long enough to prevent binding during turns and short enough to prevent dragging.

No trailer boater should ever start down the road without hooking up the safety chains. Every state but two (New Hampshire and West Virginia) requires the chains to be attached while under way. Inspect the chains before every trip with your boat. This should be part of the checklist prior to getting under way (see page 85 for the checklist).

WIRING HARNESS AND SURGE BRAKE CABLE

The final two components in the trailer/tow vehicle link are the wiring harness for the trailer lights and the surge brake cable. These are important *not* because they bear part of the load, but because they ensure that vital safety features are in working order.

The typical trailer boat wiring harness features a flat-four plug that's female except for the ground wire on the tow vehicle and male except for the ground wire on the trailer. But this is slowly beginning to change. Many tow vehicle manufacturers are using seven-pin connections and trailer manufacturers are using the same seven-pin feature in their systems more often. But chances are extremely good that you will face a seven-pin connection on the truck and a four-or five-pin connection on the trailer (if your trailer has more than four pins, it usually has brakes). What to do? Most auto shops sell adapters. But before you go looking for a seven-five or a four-six adapter, take a look at the shape of each. Some are round while others are flat. You may need to buy a four-pin flat that attaches to a five-pin round, for example.

The surge brake emergency cable is a safety system that will apply the brakes on your trailer in the event it becomes separated from the tow vehicle. The emergency cable is linked directly to the master brake cylinder; if pulled it jerks a lever, plunger assembly forward, activating it to trigger the brakes. This failsafe system is something you never want to forget to connect prior to getting under way. Yes, this too is on the checklist.

REVIEW

1 The first consideration is to determine the proper hitch class you require. It's based on the GVWR of your trailer (and this doesn't mean just the trailer, but how much weight the trailer is capable of carrying in addition to its own weight). A Class I hitch has a maximum rating of 2,000 pounds. A Class II hitch has a maximum rating of 3,500 pounds. A Class III hitch has a maximum rating of 5,000 pounds. A Class IV hitch has a maximum rating of 10,000 pounds. Don't cut this weight rating too closely. Give yourself a generous cushion even if it means moving up a class.

2 Perhaps the best recommendation for choosing a hitch is to pick one that's strong enough to match the weight rating (tow capacity) of your vehicle—even if this is heavier than the GVWR of your trailer. By doing this, if you buy a bigger boat before replacing your tow vehicle, you won't be forced to replace the hitch as well.

3 Carefully consider how the hitch attaches to the tow vehicle. The frame-mounted hitch is the best type because it has attachment points on one of the strongest components of your tow vehicle—the frame. A step-bumper hitch is also good, but only if it has frame attachment points. A bumper-frame hitch can work for light towing, but it may negate the impact-absorbing design of your bumper. A bumper-mount hitch is only acceptable for extremely light towing loads and isn't recommended for trailer boating.

4 Receiver-type hitches with removable ball-mount platforms offer trailer boaters great versatility compared to fixed ball-mount platforms, but both get the job done. Removable hitches can be stored when not in use, and can be fitted with reversible extensions to facilitate height adjustment.

5 Weight-distributing or load-equalizing hitches are often used with very heavy loads. Some tow vehicle manufacturers require them for certain load levels. Be sure to check your owner's manual before installing one.

6 Solid-steel hitch balls are recommended for all types of trailer boating. Two-piece balls may be safely used for light loads. For loads up to 2,000 pounds, a $1\frac{7}{8}$-inch hitch ball is sufficient. For loads up to 5,000 pounds, a 2-inch hitch ball is required. For loads beyond 5,000 pounds, stouter-diameter balls and ball components are required.

7 When you set up your towing rig, make sure the ball and coupler are at approximately the same height. This will prevent an excessive angle from occurring that may leave your boat or tow vehicle unbalanced and susceptible to damage. Fine height tuning can be done through the use of reversible receiver-type hitches, ball-mount extensions and replaceable ball necks. Tow the trailer as level as possible.

8 Lever-type and hand-wheel type couplers are equally suitable for trailering, but the lever-type has a trigger lock mechanism that provides an extra margin of safety.

9 Pay attention to load ranges. Your hitch has one. Your coupler has one. Know what they are and make certain you never exceed them.

CHAPTER 4

The Tow Vehicle

TOW VEHICLES ARE BIGGER, MORE POWERFUL, AND come in more plentiful styles than ever before (in 2005, there were more than 600 variations of tow vehicles available). Once high-end-only manufacturers, Mercedes Benz, Porsche, Cadillac, and Lincoln now produce sport utility vehicles with tow capacities equal to what some light trucks can pull. In fact, light trucks and SUVs now account for more than half of all new vehicles sold in the United States. This trend is expanding the towing option to more people.

What makes a good tow vehicle for a trailer boat? Well, there's no simple answer. And if you've spent much time looking at Web pages for fishermen and boaters, you'll see a lot of questions about tow vehicles.

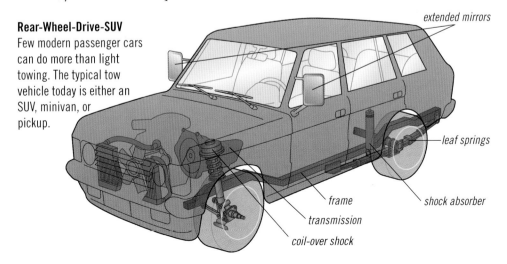

Rear-Wheel-Drive-SUV
Few modern passenger cars can do more than light towing. The typical tow vehicle today is either an SUV, minivan, or pickup.

extended mirrors

leaf springs

shock absorber

frame

transmission

coil-over shock

The search for a tow vehicle begins with a manufacturer's tow rating. This rating is based on such specifications as vehicle weight, engine size, suspension strength, rear-axle ratio, cooling capacity, whether there is a "tow package" available, transmission, drive system, and frame strength. To understand a tow rating better, it's important to know about the components and systems on which the tow vehicle's essential design is based.

TOW CAPACITY

A vehicle's tow capacity is just what it says, the maximum amount of weight that the vehicle can pull. You'll find it listed in the owner's manual or online at the vehicle manufacturer's website.

Car and truck manufacturers often list a second important tow vehicle spec: Gross Combined Weight Rating (GCWR), which is the maximum weight of both the tow vehicle and the loaded trailer—including cargo, fuel, and passengers—that the vehicle can safely handle. The GCWR minus the weight of the fully loaded tow vehicle is its towing capacity. The GCWR is usually listed on the tow vehicle manufacturer's website, as well as in the owner's manual.

You'll notice another specification called curb weight. This is the weight of the vehicle with a full tank of fuel. Curb weight doesn't include cargo, options, or passengers. Some cars and trucks are rated to tow as little as 25% of their curb weight, while others are rated to tow considerably more. In addition, you'll find that the maximum tow rating of some vehicles allows for surprisingly little additional weight for passengers and gear. In some cases, if the weight of your boat and trailer reaches the maximum tow rating, the GCWR is actually 600 pounds or less—the weight of a family of four without luggage. Take the time to figure the weight you intend your vehicle to carry and tow. You may be surprised.

Most owner's manuals also list a figure for Gross Axle Weight Rating (GAWR), which is the maximum load each axle of your tow vehicle is rated to carry. Since GAWR figures are generally very close to a fifty-fifty split between the front and rear axles, this measurement isn't a major factor for most trailer boaters, except for those with fifth wheels and rigs with heavy tongue weights.

ENGINE POWER

A popular phrase among mechanics and car buffs is "you can't beat cubic inches." This refers to the cubic-inch displacement (CID) of the cylinders inside the engine block. In simpler terms, it's engine size. This component plays a pivotal role in the engine's production of horsepower and torque—how much weight the engine can move by developing a twisting force on the drive shaft. Torque will appear in the spec sheet of the tow vehicle as pounds per foot/rpm (i.e., pounds moved one foot with the engine running at a given number of rpm). One way of explaining torque is that the more horsepower you have, the faster you can pull your boat and trailer up a hill (or a steep boat ramp), while the more torque you have determines if you can get over the hill (or up the boat ramp) in the first place.

SUSPENSION

As on the trailer, the tow vehicle's suspension system plays a significant role in trailering, especially the rear suspension. Trailer tongue weight is transferred directly onto the rear suspension, and its strength is a major determinant in a manufacturer's tongue weight and tow ratings.

To beef up the rear suspension, tow vehicles are often equipped with heavy-duty leaf springs, shock absorbers, stabilizer bars, A-arms, helper springs, trailing arms, overload springs, and air bags. With the addition of these rugged components, the tow ratings can be increased substantially.

Coil-Over Shock Suspension
Combining the best of coil springs and shock absorbers, coil-over shocks with control and trailing arms are an alternative to leaf springs for a tow vehicle's rear end.

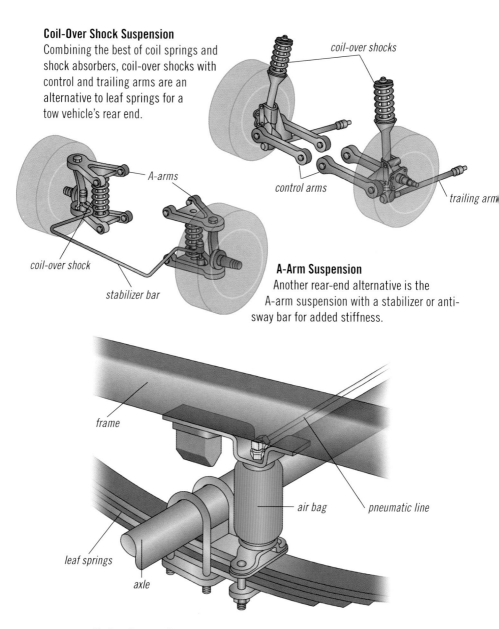

coil-over shocks

A-arms

control arms

trailing arm

coil-over shock

stabilizer bar

A-Arm Suspension
Another rear-end alternative is the A-arm suspension with a stabilizer or anti-sway bar for added stiffness.

frame

air bag

pneumatic line

leaf springs

axle

Air-bag Suspension
Adjustable air bags act as stiffening components to rear leaf springs.

The front suspension doesn't necessarily play a pivotal role in trailering; so adding heavy-duty components here won't have much of an effect on the vehicle's towing capacity. However, it makes sense to have a comparable suspension set up on both ends of the frame, so whenever the rear is beefed up, heavy-duty coil springs, shocks, coil-over shocks, stabilizer bars, and torsion bars are generally added to the front.

AXLE RATIO

Although few non-towers pay attention to axle ratio, this is one of the most important variables in trailer boating. The axle ratio represents the number of engine revolutions made for each revolution of the drive axle. For example, a mid-range axle ratio listed as 3.42 stands for 3.42 engine (or, more accurately, drive shaft) revolutions per revolution of the drive axle. Since most tow vehicles are rear-wheel drive, this is often specifically referred to as rear-axle ratio.

The axle ratio is controlled by a set of ring gears found in the differential. By changing these gears, you can directly influence torque where it's needed most—at the drive axle. With the drive shaft turning

> The higher the axle ratio, the more torque it produces.

more than three times faster than the rate of the drive wheels, the engine builds up a great amount of torque in the drive line. The higher the axle ratio, the more torque it produces. The lower the axle ratio, the less torque.

Manufacturer tow ratings are directly affected by axle ratio. A sport utility vehicle with a 2.73 axle ratio, for example, may be rated to tow only 2,000 pounds. The same sport utility vehicle equipped with the same engine and a 3.42 axle ratio may be rated for 4,000 pounds. Put a 3.73 axle ratio (very common on tow vehicles) on the vehicle and it may be rated for as much as 6,000 pounds. Some other axle ratios available on modern tow vehicles are 4.10 and 4.56, so there's a wide variety from which to choose.

Despite the fact that cars and trucks with higher axle ratios make

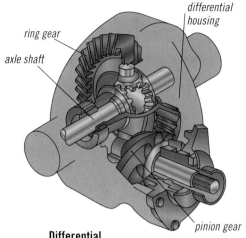

Differential
Inside the differential housing, the torque of the drive shaft is transferred to the rear axles through the pinion and ring gears.

superior tow vehicles, there's a downside too. Vehicles with high axle ratios have louder engine noise, lower top-end speed, and poorer fuel economy. For these reasons, it's a good idea to make sure your choice of axle ratio is the right one for your trailering needs.

DRIVE SYSTEMS

It makes a big difference to trailering and tow ratings if your vehicle is front-wheel drive (FWD) or rear-wheel drive (RWD). The same is true for two-wheel drive (2WD), four-wheel drive (4WD), and all-wheel drive (AWD).

Here's why: Instead of the typical drive shaft that's used in rear-wheel drive, a front-wheel drive system uses a transaxle. A transaxle is an assembly that combines the transmission, differential, and drive axle into one unit. Because transaxles are designed for use in passenger cars, they're only built for light-duty use and generally don't possess the same strength as RWD systems. Consequently, FWD systems have much lower tow ratings than RWD systems, typically much lower.

There's another drawback to FWD for towing: You encounter it on the launch ramp in the form of reduced traction. It's caused by tongue weight pressing down on the rear end of the tow vehicle and lifting, albeit slightly, the front wheels of the tow vehicle. The effect is compounded during acceleration, which also tends to shift vehicle weight to the rear. The result is a sharply reduced capacity to pull a boat out of the water, especially up steep, slippery ramps.

Another potential problem for FWD occurs while under way. If the tongue weight raises the drive wheels even slightly, the result could be reduced steering control and trailer sway. For these reasons, FWD vehicles are generally rated for light towing duty (e.g., a PWC, a personal watercraft).

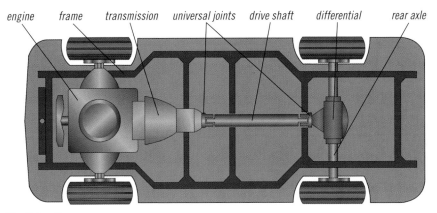

engine   frame   transmission   universal joints   drive shaft   differential   rear axle

The Drive line
The components that transfer power from the engine's crankshaft to the drive wheels comprise the driveline. Shown here is a conventional rear-wheel-drive vehicle.

To put it in a single sentence: rear-wheel drive is preferred for towing a boat. But there are two options using all of the wheels that will usually improve a tow vehicle's performance.

. . . rear-wheel drive is preferred for towing a boat.

Four-wheel drive is a benefit that results in improved traction in all conditions, which is an important feature to have on wet launch ramps. Once the 4WD system is engaged, power and torque are provided to all four wheels. This is accomplished by a series of gears, which in addition to delivering power, also provide a high and low range of operation. When the low-range gears are engaged, engine rpm increases. The result is high torque production, which comes in handy when negotiating difficult conditions.

Despite the obvious benefits of 4WD, it isn't the answer for every boater's needs. In some cases, manufacturers lower tow ratings for 4WD vehicles. The systems add weight to the vehicle, reduce top-end speed, and potentially increase maintenance costs.

All-wheel drive (AWD) and 4WD systems are similar but AWD is engaged full-time. AWD is designed for operating on slippery surfaces (e.g., the algae on the concrete of a boat ramp) and in most designs has a power ratio of 65% on the rear wheels and 35% on the front wheels in normal conditions; this will change depending on the conditions you encounter. If you drive only on dry pavement, AWD will do little to improve your towing ability.

Limited slip differential is designed to prevent one drive wheel from spinning uselessly while the other remains motionless. It does this by partially locking the right and left axle assemblies so that both turn and deliver power. Limited slip differential is available on both 2WD and 4WD vehicles. Its benefits and drawbacks are similar to those of 4WD.

TRANSMISSIONS

Quite often, experienced drivers are puzzled when they learn that manufacturers' tow ratings are generally downgraded for manual transmissions compared to automatics. There are several reasons for this. The first is that a manual transmission requires the driver to engage a clutch and physically shift between gears. Although this gives the driver tremendous control over the drive train in most situations, during trailering it puts more stress on components than they were designed to absorb. Manufacturers don't believe that clutches in passenger cars and light-duty trucks are durable enough to handle towed loads, especially when negotiating steep launch ramps. Today, large portions of the heavy-duty truck market have automatic transmissions (and some manufacturers have a special tow/haul mode position on the shift lever).

In addition to an automatic transmission's ability to shift gears automatically, it has a torque-sensing capacity that makes it ideal for adjusting to the added strain of a trailer boat. Also, drivers with automatic transmissions don't have to ride the clutch to build up torque when it's needed for pulling power. One more tip about automatic transmissions: most manufacturers recommend not towing with the transmission in overdrive. Check your owner's manual.

COOLING SYSTEMS

Nothing is more potentially damaging to hard-working vehicle parts than heat, and nothing builds it faster than pushing an engine to its limit by towing a heavy boat. To control heat buildup, typical passenger vehicles are equipped with light-duty cooling systems, which aren't suitable for towing.

A good tow vehicle's cooling system will feature beefier parts. These include a radiator with additional core layers, a radiator fan with additional blades and a thermostatic clutch, a high-performance water pump, an auxiliary transmission cooler, and engine oil cooler. The addition of these and other cooling-system parts will greatly improve a vehicle's tow rating.

FUEL

You have a choice between diesel and gasoline-powered engines. Diesels are expensive but with that added investment up front, you'll have better torque for pulling a trailer. Diesel fuel is more expensive than gasoline but in general, diesel engines are preferred for towers putting a lot of miles under their wheels. Diesel vs. gasoline is an age-old debate in the same way as bunks vs. rollers. Bottom line: the answer is whatever works best for you.

Diesel vs. gasoline is an age-old debate in the same way as bunks vs. rollers.

MANUFACTURER'S TOW PACKAGE

Perhaps the biggest single factor affecting a vehicle's tow rating is whether or not it has a manufacturer's tow package. This cluster of factory-installed trailering components is an option package available at the time of purchase and can more than double the vehicle's overall tow rating.

Here's a rundown of what's included in a typical manufacturer's tow package: heavy-duty radiator and fan, transmission and transaxle cooler, engine-oil cooler, high-performance water pump, heavy-duty turn signals, heavy-duty suspension system, factory-installed hitch, higher-ratio axle gearing, heavy-duty front brakes, high-amp alternator, heavy-duty battery, factory-installed wiring harness, and extra-wide exterior mirrors.

A manufacturer's tow package, such as the one listed above, will generally cost several hundred dollars if requested when the vehicle is ordered. To make the changes at a later time will probably cost several thousand dollars.

Oversized mirrors on a tow vehicle are popular because they allow the driver to see the boat while under way on the road and they are equally useful to see the boat trailer's position down the ramp.

REVIEW

Factors like comfort, style, performance, handling, and price are important considerations when buying a new tow vehicle. When the vehicle is intended for trailering, a whole new set of factors must be added.

1 The first three things you need to know about a tow vehicle are its tow rating, tongue-weight rating, and GCWR (gross combined weight rating). Since you already know the weight of your boat/motor/trailer, set this figure as your tow vehicle's minimum tow rating. If you haven't purchased your trailering rig yet, make your vehicle's maximum tow rating the upper limit for your rig. Be sure to leave a cushion of at least several hundred pounds in your vehicle's tow rating and GCWR for safety. Remember that tongue weight should be no more than ten percent of your rig's total weight and that the weight of passengers, luggage, and fuel must be added into the GCWR.

2 When you're presented with an engine option, the bigger the better. While under load, big engines strain less than small engines and engines that labor least, last longer. Also, remember that production of torque is more important than production of horsepower.

3 Car, truck, or SUV? Few passenger cars can handle more than light towing, if any at all. Look at tow capacity and then decide.

4 The thing to note about a rear suspension system is how it reacts to tongue weight. Make sure it provides a level ride without lifting the front end and is sturdy enough to prevent bottoming out over bumps.

5 While higher axle ratios are generally beneficial to tow vehicles, they're not the answer in all cases. A balance must be struck between the axle ratio, the size of the engine, and the weight of the towed load. Fortunately, manufacturers make this choice easy by charting tow ratings based on different axle ratios and engine sizes. One tip to keep in mind is that little will be gained by choosing an axle ratio so high that it gives you twice the towing capacity you need. In fact, a great deal may be lost in terms of regular performance.

6 Front-wheel drive or rear-wheel drive? Basically, FWD systems are designed and built for use in passenger cars. Consequently, they're not as heavy-duty as RWD. Also, the front wheels in FWD are subject to poor traction when weight is shifted to the rear during the normal course of trailering. However, FWD is suitable for many light and medium towing situations.

7 Two-wheel, four-wheel, or all-wheel? Some manufacturers lower tow ratings for vehicles equipped with 4WD—questions about durability under towing stress for long periods of time are the most common reason. Another important consideration is that 4WD has higher maintenance costs. However, nothing beats 4WD or AWD on steep, slippery launch ramps.

8 Manual or automatic transmission? The clutch is the weak link in a manual transmission. Most manufacturers don't believe it can handle the strain of trailer boating. For this reason, tow ratings for manual transmissions are often significantly lower than for automatics. An automatic transmission for the tow vehicle is the better option.

9 There's very little controversy surrounding manufacturer tow packages. Order one at the time of purchase and it will cost much, much less than buying the vehicle and adding the tow package features later.

10 Diesel or gasoline? Diesel engines cost more and diesel fuel is more expensive but these engines are preferred for trailer boaters putting high mileage on their rigs. If you are just driving to the local boat ramp, a gasoline engine will probably be the better choice.

CHAPTER 5

On the Road

 FOR THE BEGINNER, TRAILERING A BOAT OUT OF
the driveway can be a white-knuckle affair. The idea of trying to maneu-
ver around a corner, into a gas station, or down the ramp while everyone
watches can be daunting. But if your boat, trailer, and tow vehicle are properly set
up and you've taken the time to do some practice runs, before long you won't even
think about it. So the question becomes: What's a proper setup? Much of this information has been covered in previous chapters but, in this section, it will be pulled
together in the form of tips that are part of The Checklist.

You've probably heard war stories or seen first-hand evidence of trailering trips gone awry. In a worst-case scenario, a trailer can snake all over the
road and drag you places you never intended to go. The boat can shift and
become seriously unbalanced, surge brakes can malfunction, and trailers can
become unhitched. These are very real stories, and when looking back, each
begins with not preparing before going on the road.

KNOW BEFORE YOU TOW

The best way to learn is to practice backing up, braking, controlling the trailer,
and overall maneuvering in advance of your trip. A time-tested place for this is a

shopping mall parking lot on a Sunday morning; back the trailer into a specific parking space or between a pair of chairs you've brought with you.

Many boaters write out a list, encase it in plastic, carry it in the glove compartment, and pull it out while doing a walkaround before leaving home. Do this before each trip, no matter how short, no matter what excuse you may use for not doing it. Between trips, follow a regular maintenance routine. And then, when you're on the road, drive with an attentive eye and listen for possible trouble. If you do this, your trailer-boat trips will be memorable for all the right reasons.

TOW VEHICLE CHECKLIST

Every vehicle requires a certain amount of care and feeding, but none more than a tow vehicle. This is especially true if it's pulling close to the maximum tow rating. Before each trip, open the hood and check all fluid levels, including oil, coolant, transmission fluid, power steering, windshield washer, and (if necessary) battery. Then check all hoses for pliability, cracks, and leaks. Check all belts for wear and proper tension. Check the air filter for dirt.

Moving around the vehicle, check the tires for tread wear, proper inflation pressure, and the condition of the sidewalls. Then do the same for your spare. One by one, turn on the headlights, signal flashers, and brake lights. Make sure all are working. Check the fuel level and fill the tank before connecting the trailer (if your boat needs fuel too, it makes sense to fill both at the same time). Gas prices are generally lower on the road than on the water. Finally, make sure the hitch and hitch ball are wrenched tight.

After hitching up, check the road clearance beneath the back bumper. Make sure it's high enough to avoid bottoming out over bumps. Finally, make sure the tow vehicle and trailer are level or close to it when connected.

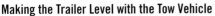

Making the Trailer Level with the Tow Vehicle

The boat trailer should be raised a little above level when being towed (bottom). If it's too low, there's a danger of safety chains being dragged while under way (top). If it's too high, there won't be enough tongue weight, which can result in dangerous swerving (middle)

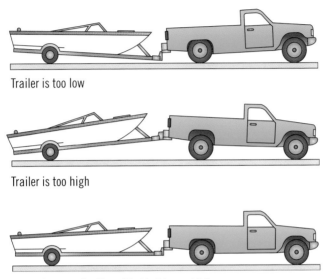

Trailer is too low

Trailer is too high

Trailer is properly aligned behind tow vehicle.

TRAILER CHECKLIST

Start at the hitch and make sure the coupler latch is properly sealed against the ball. Make sure the locking lever is in the down position and the safety pin is in place. Also, if it's a receiver-type hitch, make sure the locking bolt is in place and that it's secured by a cotter pin. If the equipment is new, make sure the ball is the right size for the coupler, and make sure all components are rated to tow the load. Finally, check all nuts and screws on the coupler to make sure they're wrenched tight.

Check the trailer's electrical connection and make sure it's tightly plugged together. For long journeys, it's a good idea to wrap electrical tape around the plug. This ensures that the plug stays connected and guards against rain. Also, for a long trip, carry a few extra bulbs if you are using incandescent lights on your trailer. Make sure all the wires are in good condition and that they're secured against chafing or dragging en route. Every other trip, make sure all the nuts and screws on the trailer are wrenched tight.

At this point, go to the tow vehicle and test the entire trailer lighting system (you may want to have someone with you who can turn on the lights and touch the brakes and operate both the turn signals and flashers while you stand outside and inspect each part of the system). Before moving on, make sure that the safety chains are crossed and secured to the hitch with shackles (instead of S hooks). Also, make sure there's enough slack to make turns, and conversely, not slack enough to drag on the ground. Finally, make sure the breakaway lanyard is attached to the hitch, and that it, too, has the proper amount of slack.

Dry Rot
Dry rot appears as small cracks in the sidewall of a boat trailer tire. Caused by ozone and accelerated by exposure to sunlight, dry rot can't be ignored once it appears on a tire.

Make sure the tongue jack has been fully raised, and if the dolly wheel or stabilizer jack is removable, make sure it's stowed for the journey. Check the winch and be certain the strap hook is tightly secured to the boat's bow eye and the brake lever is locked. Also, make sure the safety chain is hooked to the bow eye and the boat is snug up against the bow stop.

Then go to the tires and wheels. Check the tires for tread wear and proper inflation pressure and, as you've just done on the tow vehicle, inspect the sidewalls for any cuts or beginnings of dry rot. Then do the same with the trailer's spare tire. Check the wheels to make sure the lug nuts are tight and that none is missing. Finally, check the wheel bearings to make sure all are fitted with grease. Take a moment and look at the boat's hull near the axles for any presence of grease. If any is on the hull, you may have a failed bearing.

Before moving on to the boat itself, check the tie-downs to make sure they're snug and well hooked to the trailer. Take special note of any contact points that might result in chafing, and insert pads where necessary.

BOAT CHECKLIST

Walk around the trailer and check how the boat is positioned. Make sure it's level from side to side and from front to back. Look under the hull to see if the strakes and chines are properly positioned on the bunks or rollers (or both). Also, be sure that the bunks or rollers are directly beneath the transom for support. Remember that the transom should neither extend beyond the bunks or rollers nor sit far forward of them. Except in the case of lightweight loads, such as personal watercraft, canoes, or small sailing skiffs, the trailer should be a virtually perfect fit. Lower antennas, vertically mounted fishing rods, and other tall objects to avoid surprise encounters with overhead obstructions. If your boat has a bimini, most trailer boaters strongly recommend lowering it. All that canvas at 55 mph can become a sail. Sails can rip, or worse, cause the boat to move on the trailer. Besides, the aluminum support system may not be able to handle the force of wind as the boat is traveling on the interstate.

Climb inside and make sure that nothing can come loose. This includes the rigging, gear (life jackets are a common sight along highways), hatches, and especially the battery. Make sure that the stowed gear keeps the center of gravity toward the bow. Do you have all the necessary Coast Guard

Keep in mind that boat tops are designed for cruising speeds on the water, not the rigors of high-speed roadway trailering. Take down any fabric top and side curtains and secure them so that they won't be damaged.

equipment aboard (flares, horn, enough life jackets for every passenger)? Do you have all the necessary keys? Do you have the plug (if applicable)?

Check the fuel and all of the oil levels and then decide whether you should replenish on the road or at the marina. Don't forget to tighten all lids. If you have a canvas cover, it's more fuel efficient to have the cover on while on the road (don't confuse the canvas cover with the bimini, though—a bimini can act like a sail at 55 mph so if it can be lowered, do so). Also, check the transom tie-downs (and carry an extra one in the event it's needed).

BASIC DRIVING TECHNIQUES

Trailering isn't hard to do, but it requires more work than simply driving a car. So it's a good idea to drive only when you're rested, and on long trips, plan to log fewer hours on the road than you normally would. It also requires serious adjustment of basic driving skills. Any time a trailer is hitched to a vehicle, normal handling characteristics are altered, and the driver must respond accordingly. The most important tip: Allow yourself time to react, and the best way to do this is to slow down.

Allow yourself time to react, and the best way to do this is to slow down.

Slower speeds give you more time to react to changing road conditions. With several thousand pounds attached to your backside, you need every second you can get. Between you and the vehicle you're following, allow at least one length of your complete rig (tow vehicle plus trailer) for every 10 mph of your speed. Stay in the right and middle lanes. Note any sluggishness in acceleration, and allow extra space for merging and passing.

Generally speaking, develop a good overall sense of anticipation. Begin reacting to posted hazards, such as sharp curves, merging traffic, narrow bridges, detours, and bumps as far in advance as possible. Now more than ever it's important to observe conditions as far down the road in front of you as possible.

A tip to keep in mind that's related to speed has to do with the overdrive setting of an automatic transmission. Stay out of it. The engine generates relatively little torque in overdrive, and manufacturers recommend against using it.

Aside from slowing down, moving safely through sharp corners is the next most important task. Remember that you must swing wide through turns to accommodate the extra length of the trailer (watch a semi truck driver make a turn in an intersection). Don't begin turning the steering wheel until you're slightly beyond the corner. If you forget, the trailer may run over a curb—or worse.

Braking is the next most important consideration. Even after leaving extra space between you and other traffic, keep in mind that towing a trailer dramatically increases the distance required to stop. This is true despite the fact that your trailer may be equipped with surge or electric brakes.

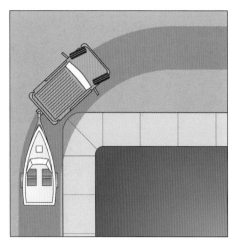

Narrow Turn Trailers take a narrower radius through turns than tow vehicles. Drivers who forget this often run over curbs.

Wider Turn Swinging wide through turns will ensure that your trailer and boat get safely around the corner.

Ideally, when you need to use the brakes you'll have time to apply them properly. Tap the brake pedal gently and then pump it harder as you gradually slow down. This will ensure a smooth and predictable stop. Even in emergency panic-stop situations, your trailer is designed to maintain a safe and predictable line behind your vehicle.

Still, anything can happen in an emergency, including a poorly secured boat's climbing over the top of a winch stand. So give yourself the best chance for success by making sure the trailer brakes are properly adjusted. They should be set neither too strong nor too light. Too strong means they lock up whenever steady pressure is applied to the brake pedal. Too light means they don't kick in until you slam the brake pedal to the floor.

Trailer brakes should be activated between these extremes at the point where hard braking begins. Interestingly, when well-adjusted trailer brakes are activated, they actually help slow the tow vehicle from the back end and give the driver an enhanced feeling of control. Poorly adjusted trailer brakes, on the other hand, can result in jackknifing. Bottom line: If you are unsure about making the adjustment yourself, take the trailer to a professional and have it done right the first time. If it isn't, there may not be a second time.

Finally, take special care climbing and descending hills. Hill climbing causes your engine, transmission, differential, and wheels to generate more than normal heat. Watch your gauges carefully up long hills, especially during hot weather. On the downside of the hill, shift into lower gears instead of using your brakes to control descent. Remember that overheated brakes are subject to fade. Brake fade is the result of long and excessive braking applications. Going downhill is one example, starting and stopping at high speeds is another. Heat builds up and can affect brake pads (the material begins to melt at temperatures above 700 degrees F). Brake fluid may also become overheated in the calipers which can result in bubbles being emitted through the brake line system. This too, will cause brake fade. Ventilated disc brakes have fewer instances of brake fade than drum brakes.

BACKING UP

The first piece of advice to keep in mind when backing up a trailer is to relax. The second is to practice, especially with a friend who can act as an observer. You don't want to try backing down a boat ramp for the first time at 10 o'clock on a summer Saturday morning while 20 other boaters wait for you to launch.

To some trailer boaters, backing down a launch ramp is the single most stressful time of the entire trip. It doesn't have to be. Start by building the necessary skills the right way. During off hours, go to the mall parking lot and spend some time getting the feel of your rig. Then, go to the boat ramp during off hours (i.e., not on a Saturday morning) and do a run-through there.

At first, simply get a feel for the rig's turning radius, its length, width, and the new experience of relying on (and trusting) side mirrors, especially the tricky right side mirror. Start off by making several turns in an increasingly tighter radius. Learn how the trailer follows the tow vehicle. Then, carefully and slowly, turn the steering wheel fully to the left and then fully to the right. Find out the points where the angle between the tow vehicle and the trailer is so sharp that they make contact with each other. Mentally

When positioning at a ramp, remember that the trailer always backs in the direction opposite to that of the car. Take the time to practice in an empty lot before heading to the launch ramp.

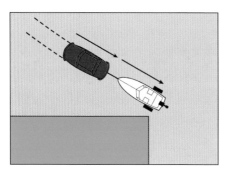

As you approach in reverse, swing close to the ramp.

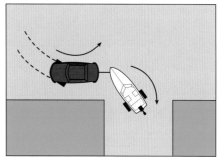

Then cut the car wheels toward the right. As the car swings slightly to the left, the trailer angles toward the ramp.

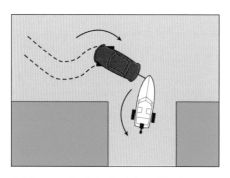

Cut the car wheels to the left and back slowly into the ramp as the trailer moves to the right.

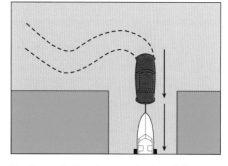

Finally, straighten the car wheels to follow the trailer as it backs down the ramp.

note these points and avoid them to prevent vehicle and trailer damage.

Now it's time to assume the basic backing-up hand position. Place one hand on the bottom of the steering wheel. With your hand in this position,

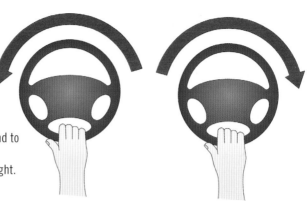

Hand Position for Backing Up
To make it easier to learn to back up with a trailer, start with your hand resting on the bottom of the steering wheel. If the trailer needs to go to the left, rotate your hand to the left. If it needs to go to the right, rotate your hand to the right.

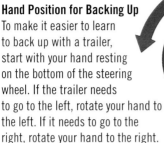

move it in the direction you want the trailer to go (i.e., if the trailer should move right, turn the bottom of the wheel toward the right). It's that simple, at least in theory.

A special note to owners of trailers with surge brakes: Don't keep your foot pressed on the throttle in reverse if the engine's racing and you're not making any progress. Poorly adjusted surge brakes are sometimes activated when the trailer is backed up, especially when going uphill. Modern surge brakes are designed to prevent this from occurring, but an occasional adjustment may be needed.

On the launch ramp, with your hand placed confidently at the bottom of the steering wheel, the first thing to remember is to go slowly. This will allow you time to minimize wandering and make timely corrections. Push the throttle gently and move your hand in the direction you want to go. Once under way, you can move your hands to a comfortable position and make small adjustments to enable the tow vehicle to follow the trailer. However, if the trailer starts heading where you don't want it to go, then stop immediately. You may want to put the tow vehicle in Forward and return to your original starting point. Sometimes, trying to straighten out the course of an already crooked trailer just isn't worth the effort. And other times, it's just plain impossible to do.

...set yourself up whenever possible to back the trailer to the left.

One good tip to remember is to set yourself up whenever possible to back the trailer to the left. Why? The reason is that the driver's seat is located on the left and you can get a full view of what's happening simply by turning around and looking out the window. When backing to the right, you're forced to rely on the right side mirror, which requires practice. You won't be able to back up to the left every time, but do it whenever you can. It tends to make life easier.

Finally, take note of how much input the steering wheel requires to turn the trailer. In general, short trailers require less steering input than long ones. The deciding factor is the distance between the trailer axle and the hitch. Short trailers tend to jackknife easily. Long ones tend to be more forgiving. So the best advice is to take an easy-does-it approach and provide no more input than necessary. And, as mentioned above, that may mean starting over at the top of the ramp.

MEETING SPECIAL CHALLENGES

One area of special concern for trailer boaters is the right side of the vehicle, which can often be a blind spot. To help cope with this problem, make sure the tow vehicle's mirrors are the right ones for the job. They should extend out and away from the tow vehicle far enough to provide an unobstructed view of the boat, which is very important for monitoring the load's progress, plus observing the inside lane of traffic, which is important for switching lanes. This may require the use of supplemental equipment, such as oversized mirrors, extension brackets, and a convex spot mirror. Go this extra mile, even if it isn't mandated by law in your state. It could make a difference in a tight situation.

Among the first things trailer boaters will notice on the road is that automobile drivers seem oblivious to your special needs. In addition to riding in the blind spot, they'll cut you off, tailgate, slow down in the middle of a steep climb, and perform a number of other equally challenging maneuvers. Despite this apparent lack of courtesy, trailer boaters need to keep a level head at all times. With a boat in tow your options are limited. Simply adjust to each situation as it arises, and keep making progress toward your destination. Road rage isn't going to get you on the water sooner. Besides, once you do arrive, it will all be worthwhile.

TRAILER SWAY

To a certain extent, all trailers sway, which means they have a tendency to wander from side to side while under way. However, occasional sway and excessive sway are two completely different things. Occasional sway is normal. Excessive sway is the trailer boater's worst nightmare.

A typical example of sway occurs when the trailer is disturbed from its normal course by a gust of wind, a passing semitruck, or bumps in the road. During this kind of sway, the trailer may lurch and then resume its normal course.

A more troublesome kind of sway occurs when the trailer develops a fishtail motion that remains constant at highway speeds. This is a warning that all is not well with your towing rig. It may not worsen to the point of becoming dangerous, but there's no guarantee it won't. If steady sway occurs while you're driving, start planning an immediate course of action. Slow down to a speed that diminishes some of the motion. Do this by letting up on the accelerator instead of using the brakes. Then look for a suitable place to pull over and inspect your rig.

The problem with trailer sway is that it may eventually worsen into a more serious condition called growing or excessive sway, where the side-to-

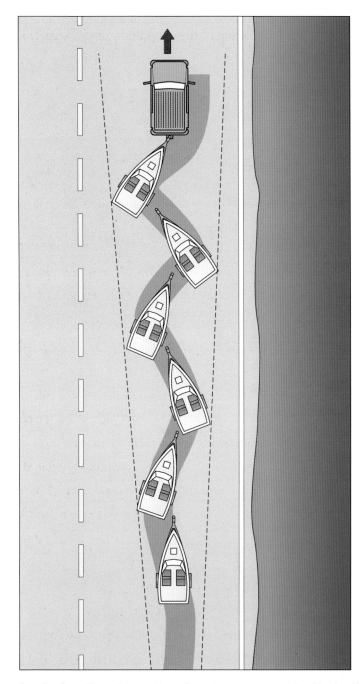

Growing Sway The serious problem of growing sway occurs when the duration of sway increases with each swing of the trailer. Eventually, a trailer prone to growing sway may take control of a tow vehicle.

ON THE ROAD ⚓ *83*

side motion increases with each swing of the pendulum. In this scenario, the trailer can take control of the tow vehicle, with disastrous results.

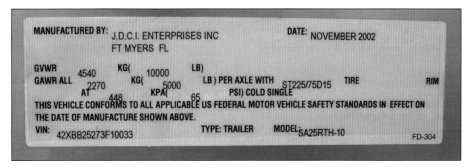

Maximum weight ratings for the trailer, axle, tongue, coupler, and hitch should be double checked against information printed on trailer labels.

Tongue weight that's either too heavy or too light, or a load that's too heavy for the tow vehicle, typically causes both steady and excessive sway. Other causes are a short wheelbase or a long overhang on the tow vehicle. But before reaching these dire conclusions, it's a good idea to start by inspecting for the following easy-to-fix problems.

Look at the trailer tires first to make sure they're properly inflated. Then inspect the trailer/tow-vehicle contact points. Make sure the ball is fully seated and locked in the coupler. Then make sure the coupler is solidly bolted to the trailer tongue. On the opposite end, be certain that the hitch is firmly welded to the tow-vehicle frame. For good measure, grab the trailer tongue and hitch firmly, and shake. What you learn by doing this will be important, but it won't necessarily solve the problem.

As mentioned earlier, significant trailer sway is usually caused by one of two fundamental problems: light tongue weight or a load that's too heavy for the vehicle. These problems are difficult to fix while under way. Check to see that the boat is resting properly on the trailer bed. If it has moved backward during the trip, use the winch to pull it back in place. Then check the boat's fuel and water levels. Are the tanks located behind the trailer's axle? Are they more full this time than usual? If so, jettisoning the water (8.3 pounds/gallon) may help. Jettisoning the fuel (about 6 pounds/gallon) must be done by filling dedicated fuel cans.

If the tongue weight is less than 7% of your trailer weight with the boat, then the boat is going to have to be moved forward on the trailer to increase the weight of the tongue on the hitch. This may involve moving the winch post forward or it may involve moving the trailer axle backward. If the tongue weight is more than 10% of your trailer weight with the boat, this too can be the cause of the excessive sway. In either case, fixing the tongue weight probably won't be accomplished while on the side of the road. And if it was proper on other travels, then you should continue to inspect all the other possible causes of excessive sway.

At this point, it's wise to double-check all your weight ratings and make sure no limits have been exceeded. Legally, you cannot tow a load that's too heavy for a vehicle's maximum rating. Is this your fundamental problem? If so, a new vehicle or a new boat is in order.

In addition to sway, a load that presses too heavily on the rear suspension will cause two other problems for drivers: potential damage to the suspension and mushy steering, which are the result of the front wheels being lifted slightly into the air. Solutions here are stiffening the rear suspension or adjusting the trailer axle to achieve a lighter tongue weight.

. . . pull over occasionally to check the rig, even if nothing is apparently wrong.

One final on-the-road tip: After you've gone through all of the pretrip safety checks and you've begun an extended trip, it's always a good idea to pull over occasionally to check the rig, even if nothing is apparently wrong. In fact, it's a good idea to do a quick status check every time you stop (for fuel or to use a rest room or just to take a break). Be sure to check the air pressure and heat of the tires and the wheel hubs. If the hubs are excessively hot, it could be a sign of improper lubrication or a signal that the surge brake is engaging frequently. Be sure to inspect the hitch and coupler, too. The sooner you discover a problem, the easier it is to fix.

The problems discussed in this section are not necessarily the norm for trailer boating. But it's a good idea to be aware of what can go wrong and know the potential solutions.

THE CHECKLIST

Do a walk around your rig with this checklist in hand. Don't assume everything is as you left it.

1 Hitch secured to the coupler and locked into place.

2 Safety chains are crisscrossed beneath the trailer tongue and secured to the tow vehicle and trailer with screw-pin shackles.

3 Trailer dolly jack attached to the tongue and folded/raised with enough clearance from the pavement.

4 Trailer tire lug nuts are tight. Trailer tires have proper inflation, tire tread is good, and tire sidewalls are in good condition (no dry rot or punctures).

5 Bearings are properly lubricated.

6 Boat-trailer and tow-vehicle lights are operating.

7 Check equipment in the boat and ensure it won't be blown out while under way, possibly hitting the windshield of a following vehicle.

8 Spare tire for the trailer? Does the jack fit the trailer?

9 Do a check of the brakes. Listen for grinding sounds when brakes are applied.

10 Drain plug and keys; remove the plug while under way so water can run out, but remember to replace it once you arrive at the boat ramp. Do you have the keys to the boat with you or are they in the ignition?

CHAPTER 6

On the Water

MOST TRAILER-BOAT STORIES INVOLVE SOMEONE making a bad decision at the boat ramp. The result has been described as modern-day slapstick comedy, with missing drain plugs, mistakes backing a trailer down a ramp, propellers and skegs dragged over concrete, tow vehicles going into the water (some with, some without a driver) and people's reactions to these (and other) situations.

If you're involved, the humor may be missing. If you're an observer, it's entertaining because the dents, dings, drenching, and damage to the ego (and boat and trailer) are entirely preventable. But at every boat ramp, if someone is having a problem, someone else is usually willing to assist in whatever way they can. If something goes wrong, yes, you'll be the topic of conversation. But if something goes really wrong, you're going to have many hands willing to help solve the problem.

There are two keys to successful boat launching and retrieving: practice and preparation. Practice, as indicated in the last chapter, means going to an empty parking lot (school or shopping mall) and getting the feel of driving with a trailer. Specifically, familiarize yourself with how the load affects engine responsiveness and braking, how it requires adjustment for extra length and width, and how it alters the fundamentals of cornering, backing up, and negotiating tight spaces. After a few hours you'll be ready for step two: preparation.

PRELAUNCH PREPARATION

The first thing to do after arriving at the launch ramp is to find a place away from the bustle of the main launching area. This is where you prepare the boat. It's a matter of courtesy, too; making other boaters wait in line because you are at the bottom of the ramp doing things that could have been done while waiting in line to launch or in a section away from the main launch area is not just inefficient—it's rude.

Start by taking the tie-downs and canvas cover off the boat and stowing them away. Did you fill the boat's fuel tank before arriving? If not, make a stop at the gas dock your first priority. This is the time to move everything from the tow vehicle to the boat, such as coolers, extra clothing, towels, sunscreen, cassettes/CDs/DVDs, fishing equipment, and so forth. Performing these tasks now will maximize your time on the water and minimize your time at the launch ramp.

Next, unhook the winch-stand safety chain from the bow eye. However, leave the winch line or strap engaged until the boat is in the water (many boat-ramp stories are about a boat sliding off the trailer as it is backed down the ramp because the winch-stand safety chain was removed). Insert and tighten all drain plugs (more stories). Disconnect the tow-vehicle/trailer wiring harness to prevent potential shorting. Then pull two docking lines out and tie them to the deck cleats. Finally, check your trailer's

One of the first pre-launch duties is to replace the transom drain plug. Establish a pre-launch checklist to make your routine on the ramp as simple and easy as possible.

wheel bearings to make sure they're fully packed with grease and have cooled down, especially if you've descended some hills to get to the water. Hubs will be cool about fifteen minutes after the journey.

RAMP INSPECTION

Even if you're familiar with the launch ramp, it's a good idea to walk over and give it a visual inspection. Conditions and water levels can change dramatically between boat trips.

Check to see if you can back in in a straight line to the water or if you have to come in at an angle. If at an angle, your best approach is to keep the water to your left when pulling in past the ramp. This enables you to back up to the left and allows you to inspect your progress by looking out the driver side window. Backing up to the right forces you to rely on the right side mirror. Before walking down the ramp, find out where you can park the tow vehicle and trailer after launching.

Now use a critical eye to evaluate the ramp itself. Is it steep? Is it slippery as a result of algae growth at the water's edge? Is it wide enough to accommodate more than one trailer? If so, is one side better than the other? Are there rocks or other obstacles in the water? Is there a drop-off at the end of the ramp and is it marked so that you can see it while backing down? Is there a strong current or a gusting wind? Is the ramp in a tidal area and, if so, how will conditions (e.g., water depth) change throughout the day? Finally, check out the location and conditions of the dock where you'll tie up after launching.

LAUNCH PROCEDURE

With tow vehicle and trailer ready, place one hand at the bottom of the steering wheel and slowly back down the ramp. Have an observer watch your progress and signal when the boat and trailer are immersed in the water. The trailer is correctly immersed when the boat slightly floats at the aft end. Note the water level on the trailer wheels and use that as a marker for future launchings. For some trailers, the wheels will be halfway submerged. For others, the wheels may be fully submerged.

Now, turn the tow-vehicle engine off and use the emergency brake and transmission to hold the vehicle in place. To be extra cautious, chock the rear wheels of the tow vehicle. Walk back to the trailer, flip the winch lever lock lever to the open position, and wind out some line. At this point, especially for those with light craft or roller trailers, the boat can slide off the trailer and be tied up at the dock.

If the boat doesn't slide off the trailer bed at this point, don't worry about it. Most modern trailers are designed for drive-on/drive-off use, which means that marine power can be used for the final "push." But be aware that "power launching" and "power retrieval" aren't allowed at a number of boat ramps throughout the country out of concern that the edge of the ramp can be damaged by the backwash of propellers undermining the sand/gravel/bottom. If you choose to "power launch," once the trailer is in place and the winch line is unhooked, the boat driver needs to press the trim button (if it is an I/O), submerge the prop, and start the engine. Then, with just a bump or two on the throttle, slowly back the boat off the trailer. If the trailer is in top condition and well matched to the boat, the tow-vehicle driver shouldn't have to assist with a push to get the boat off. But a light shove or two doesn't hurt when necessary. Now pull the trailer out of the ramp area.

There are two important things to keep in mind if you do a power launch: (1) Be sure to set the trim so that the engine's lower unit is deep enough to submerge the prop and water pickups but not so deep that the prop is in danger of striking the bottom; (2) Make sure the engine is warmed up and running properly before backing off the trailer. You don't want the engine to go dead in the water the very second the boat is out of reach. To do it properly, let the engine run a minute while checking the oil pressure and flow of water through the cooling system.

If you don't use the engine to get the boat off the trailer, have one person in the boat while another stands on the trailer tongue and pushes. This is where having a good long bow line is handy so that the boat can be pulled over to the dock. If you're launching by yourself, keep the bow line in hand after the boat is afloat. The reason is all too obvious.

One special reminder for inboard and stern-drive power boaters: Don't forget to purge the engine compartment of fumes before turning the ignition key. In fact, it's a good idea to open the engine hatch and turn on the blower before dropping the boat in the water. This is especially important after long trailer journeys, which may cause fuel to slosh around and build up fumes.

When the tow vehicle and boat go their separate ways, the tow-vehicle driver heads for a good parking spot while the boat driver heads for a nearby

Make sure that you have inspected the ramp before you line up to use it; make any last-minute checks. If you are not familiar with the ramp, take time to talk to someone who has just used it and learn of any peculiarities or problem aspects.

Line up the car and trailer, then back the rig down the ramp as described in the text.

While a crewmember disconnects the bow hitch cable, one or two others control the boat with lines attached at the bow and stern.

Make sure that one or two crewmembers have hold of the bow and stern lines before giving the boat a light push to float it off the trailer.

Make the boat fast temporarily while parking the vehicle and trailer. In this illustration, the trailer is still in the water, showing how far it needs to enter the water in order to launch the boat.

dock to tie up. Both drivers should move at sensible speeds, but dawdling is discouraged. Remember, others are waiting to use the facilities.

Sound difficult? It isn't. With a little practice the entire procedure—from prepping to launching—takes less than ten minutes.

DOCK MANEUVERING

As mentioned earlier, the first thing to do after launching is to tie your boat up to a nearby dock. One tip to keep in mind is that, given the option of

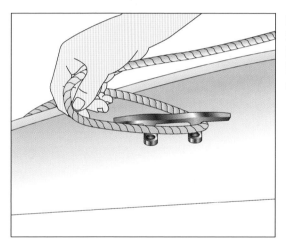

Cleating a Line
Start by looping the line around the base of the cleat. This will help relieve some of the stress on the knot.

Cross the line over the cleat and loop around one of the cleat horns.

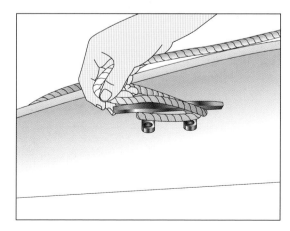

After rounding the horn, crisscross the line over the cleat.

Make a loop in the line, twist it, and place it over the horn.

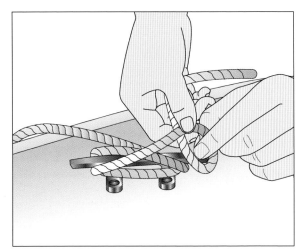

Now pull it tight. It's quicker and easier to tie than to explain.

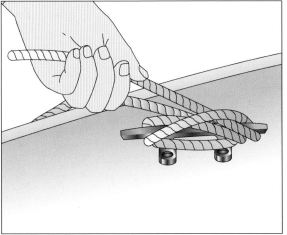

tying onto either side of the dock, use the most windward side or the dock that is most up-current. It's easier on your boat if you dock into the wind because the hull won't be pushed against the side of the dock. Using the dock that is up-current from the boat ramp will have the same effect. When you tie up on the leeward (or downwind) side, the wind pushes the boat into the dock and causes unnecessary wear and tear.

An easy way to tie your boat up to a cleat on the dock is to use a figure-eight knot. Take the end of the line and run it completely around the base of the cleat. Then come up and over the near horn. Cross over the cleat on the way to the far horn and go down and around it. On the way back to the near horn, crisscross the line. Finally, finish it off with a half hitch and pull taut. It's one of the fastest and most effective knots in boating.

Pulling into a dock or a slip requires a bit of boat-driving skill, even at idle speed. The first thing you'll notice is that a boat, unlike a car, steers from the stern. When you turn the steering wheel, the stern moves rather than the bow. The second thing you'll notice is that a moving boat, especially if it's equipped with outboard or stern-drive power, only responds to steering input when the engine is in gear. In neutral, the steering wheel is mostly useless. For this reason, a good skipper will use a combination of steering adjustments and small bursts of power to glide toward a dock.

The best method for docking is to set up a straight-line approach at about a 30-degree angle. As the bow approaches, turn the wheel away from the dock and shift into neutral. This action will tend to swing the stern around parallel with the dock. When the boat is a few feet away, turn the steering wheel all the way over in the direction of the dock, shift into reverse, and give the throttle a brief burst. This will do two things: it will stop the boat's forward progress and it will pull the stern in close for tying up.

After all passengers and supplies are aboard, it's time to pull away from the dock and head out for a day of boating adventure. First, start the

Stern Steering

Unlike a car, a boat steers from the stern. Although the line of approach taken by the boat driver enables the bow to clear the obstacle, the stern isn't so lucky.

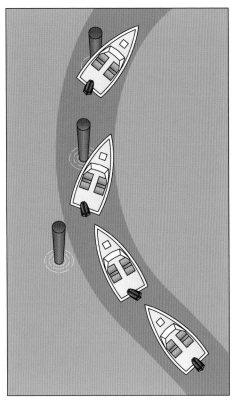

When brought in uncomfortably close to an obstacle, the boat should be straightened out first and then steered at a shallow exit angle.

Pulling into Dock

The best way to pull into a dock is to idle in slowly at an angle.

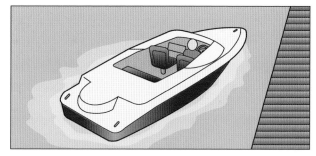

When you approach the dock closely, shift the throttle into neutral.

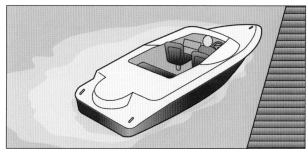

While in neutral, turn the steering wheel in the direction of the dock as far as it will go and shift into reverse.

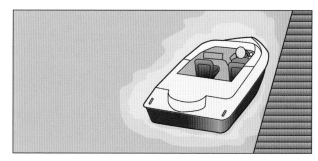

With the steering wheel turned toward the dock and the throttle in reverse the prop will complete the maneuver by pulling the stern into the dock.

engine and make sure it's warmed up and running properly. Then get a deckhand to untie the lines and push the bow away from the dock. Shift into forward and pull away from the dock at idle speed. Make sure you don't turn the wheel too sharply or you will send the stern banging into the

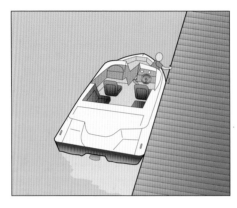

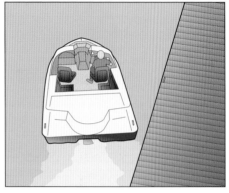

Pulling Away From Dock
With little wind or current to worry about, the first steps are to untie all lines and push off from the bow.

Now properly angled, idle away from the dock. It's a good idea to go a safe distance before turning the wheel sharply.

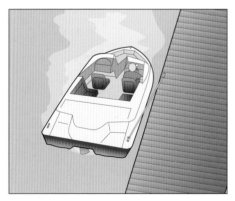

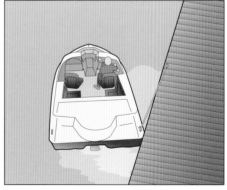

When wind or current make getting the bow away from the dock a problem, start by tying a line to the stern cleat as shown above.

Then turn the steering wheel toward the dock and shift into reverse. This maneuver will swing the bow free of the dock. Now untie the line, shift into forward gear and pull away. Make sure to use a fender at the stern of the boat when the dock is without padding.

dock. Take a narrow departure angle and hold it until you are safely away from the dock. Then you can turn as sharply as you like.

Adjusting to the wind or current is as important in leaving a dock as it is in approaching one. If you're heading out into the wind or current, you may have a hard time getting the bow out far enough to pull away safely. In these conditions, your best bet is to put a fender between the stern of your boat and the dock. Then untie all the dock lines except for one, a spring line that's cleated amidships on the dock and leading to a cleat on the stern. Now you're ready to get under way.

Turn the wheel all the way toward the dock and shift into reverse. Use enough throttle to pivot the bow well into the wind or current. Then shift into neutral and quickly untie the spring line. With the bow pointed well away from the dock, shift into forward and head safely out of the marina. Remember not to turn too sharply until the boat is well away from the dock.

BOAT HANDLING

Numerous books have been written on the subject of boat handling. A word of advice: read one. There's no substitute for being well versed in this complex subject. Even better, take one of many boating courses offered around the country (the U.S. Coast Guard Auxiliary website is www.cgaux.org/cgauxweb/classes/master.shtml, while the U.S. Power Squadron classes can be found at www.usps.org). Classes offered by these organizations may require a minimal fee. For free operating information, contact the BoatU.S. Foundation at www.boatus.com.

In addition to the skills already discussed in this chapter, boaters need to know the rules of the road regarding rights of way on the water. They need to know how to cope with hazards, identify marker buoys, tie knots, and handle emergencies. They also need to be familiar with basic troubleshooting

techniques, towing procedures, navigation, anchoring, heavy-weather seamanship, and much more.

Two of the best and most comprehensive books available on the subject of boating are *Chapman's Piloting: Seamanship & Small Boat Handling*
by Elbert S. Maloney, and *Stapleton's Powerboat Bible* by Sid Stapleton. Both
are one-stop reference books published by Hearst Marine Books.

Effects of Engine Trim

With the prop tucked all the way under, the boat will quickly pop up on plane. However, unless adjusted, it will deliver a sluggish, bow-down ride.

Power-robbing rooster tails and squirrelly handling are the result of excessively high prop trimming. Engine damage may also occur if insufficient water is fed to the pickups.

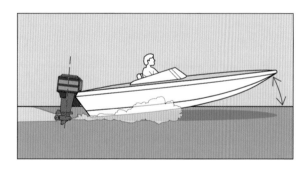

When the prop is correctly trimmed, the boat rides with a level attitude and the bow stays efficiently out of the water.

HAULING OUT AND RETRIEVING

As you might expect, the correct procedure for hauling out a boat is basically the reverse of launching it. Pull up to the dock and let all ashore who are going ashore, especially the tow-vehicle driver. Then, either tie up at the dock or find a place to idle and wait until the tow-vehicle driver backs the trailer into the water.

Two tips for the tow-vehicle driver: (1) Make sure the trailer backs straight into the water, otherwise the boat may not be able to position itself correctly in the cradle of the trailer; (2) Make sure the waterline intersects the trailer wheels at roughly the same points as during launching.

Now, the tow-vehicle driver engages the emergency brake, shifts the transmission into Park to help hold the vehicle in place, and signals the boat driver to pull onto the trailer. If you are not going to power load, then the driver and crew stand ready to assist in bringing the boat properly onto the trailer, attaching the winch line to the bow eye, and cranking the winch to secure the boat in place. However, if you are going to power load, the driver will shift the boat into gear, trim the prop up to prevent striking the bottom, and idle toward the trailer (don't go fast but maintain forward motion). It's important that the driver approach on a straight line and make as few steering corrections as possible. If the boat is heading for an off-center approach, it's best to start over.

When the bow comes to rest on the trailer bed, the tow-vehicle driver must evaluate whether or not the boat is properly seated on the bunks or rollers. If it isn't seated correctly, then the boat must be backed off the trailer and pulled in again. Some trailers have accessories called guideposts attached to either side of the trailer's back that can be used to line the boat up even if the trailer is under water. No boat should be towed when it's misaligned on the trailer. Now, the tow-vehicle driver must determine how close the bow is to the winch stand. If it's nudged up to the bow stop, then the driver may simply hook the winch line and crank the winch handle (or engage the electric winch) so that the boat is snug against the winch post. If the bow is several inches away from the winch stand, then the boat driver must shift into forward and bump the throttle to move the boat closer. When the proper position is achieved, the tow-vehicle driver hooks up the winch line and secures the boat to the trailer.

Once the boat is securely in place, the boat driver should turn off the engine and tilt the lower unit completely out of the water. The final step is to attach the winch-stand safety chain. Remember that the weight of the boat alone isn't enough to hold it in the trailer bed. Many boats have been dropped on the launch ramp because they weren't properly secured. Also, now is the time to crank the winch tight and flip the safety latch. If you've chocked the wheels, make sure you remove the chocks. Otherwise, you're not going to go very far.

The tow-vehicle driver will shift into low gear and pull slowly but firmly up the ramp. If the marina/launch facility has a washdown area, this should be your first stop. Remove the drain plug to let out any extra water and then proceed to give both the boat and trailer a thorough spraying. In many areas around the country, boaters at launch facilities are asked to pay attention to ANS (aquatic nuisance species) that may have attached themselves to the trailer or the boat hull (a good website is www.anstaskforce.gov). This includes zebra mussels (now common in the Great Lakes), round goby, and hydrilla. A washdown area at the marina/boat ramp is helpful in getting these hitchhikers off the boat and trailer surfaces so they can't be carried to another body of water and become a nuisance there. Besides checking for ANS, flush out the engine's cooling system, and if your trailer has a water washdown for the brake system, hook the hose to it now (otherwise, do this at home).

Finally, check that the boat is properly aligned on the trailer and make sure the tie-downs have been secured. After a long day on the water, it's tempting to hurry through the final procedures for stowing gear, covering the boat, and securing it to the trailer. Certainly, there's less joy leaving a marina than arriving, but you won't savor the experience unless all trailer-boat responsibilities are properly and safely executed. Bottom line: This doesn't take long to do at all and the peace of mind is worth it.

Checking that the boat safety chain is hooked to the bowline is an important security step before hitting the road.

Before getting back under way after hauling out, crank the winch tight and flip on the safety latch.

REVIEW

1 When you arrive at a ramp with which you're not familiar, take the time to walk its length and inspect it for holes as well as length. The end of some ramps will be marked along the dock.

2 If you are waiting in a line to use the ramp, this is the time to prepare for the launch. Move the coolers and equipment from the tow vehicle to the boat, take off the cover, and remove the tie-down straps, but keep the boat attached to the trailer with the bow eye and winch strap. If you do all of this at the bottom of the ramp, you are wasting everyone else's time because it could have been done earlier.

3 Put the plug in prior to launching. There are too many boat-ramp stories based on a forgotten plug.

4 If you make a mistake backing down the ramp, it's usually easier to simply drive back up and start over.

5 Put one hand on the bottom of the steering wheel. This is considered the easiest way to steer the trailer down the ramp because, in this position, the trailer will move in the direction you move your hand.

6 In general, the maximum water level should be no more than half the height of the boat-trailer wheels. If the tow-vehicle tires are also deeply immersed, consider putting a longer tongue on the trailer.

7 Your boat steers differently than the tow vehicle. When you turn the wheel of a boat, the stern moves instead of the bow.

8 Maneuvering is also affected by the wind and the current. If possible, dock your boat "downwind" so that the wind first crosses the dock before crossing your boat. This will keep the tied-up boat away from the dock and prevent unnecessary wear and tear on the hull.

9 Loading your boat on the trailer is usually the reverse of what you do when launching. When the boat is on the trailer, winch it the remaining distance to the trailer's winch post. Be sure to attach the winch-stand safety chain.

10 Before going out on the highway, go through the checklist. Make sure the boat is secure.

CHAPTER 7

Maintenance

 FOR MANY OF US, THE ERA OF CLIMBING UNDER the family vehicle or poking extensively beneath the hood is pretty much over. Certain small jobs can often still be performed, but for the most part, modern cars and trucks—and their onboard computers, fuel-injection systems, and an undercarriage that's crisscrossed with stabilizers, A-arms, and torsion bars—are now well beyond the maintenance ability of most weekend mechanics.

This isn't necessarily the case with trailers, tow hitches, boats, and some marine engines. In fact, frequent inspection and hands-on maintenance are the norm for the majority of trailer boaters. Not only will these tasks save you money and ensure that everything is in top operating condition, they'll guarantee that your equipment preserves its value for future resale.

There are many ways to approach trailer-rig maintenance, and a good one is to start at the ground, with the tires and wheels, and then work up to the trailer, the hitch, and the boat.

TIRES AND WHEELS

The first thing to do here is to check the maximum capacity rating for your trailer tires. This information is stamped on the sidewalls. Multiply the rating figure by the number of tires on the trailer, and then make sure the total is equal to or greater than the load (the weight of the boat, trailer, and equipment). Maintaining a safety margin of a few hundred pounds is recommended.

Next, check the inflation pressure on the tires and make sure it, too, complies with the stamped sidewall information. This inspection should be done frequently, because a fully loaded trailer should never run with underinflated tires. Underinflation causes overheating, which leads to premature wear and blowouts. If you notice the edges of the tire tread show more wear than the center, the tire is underinflated. Overinflation, meanwhile, can cause the tread to disintegrate. If the center of the tread shows more wear than the edges, the tire is overinflated. Every tire manufacturer will urge that inflation be done when the tire is cold.

Now it's time to inspect each tire, including the spare, for signs of excessive wear, both in the tread area and in the sidewalls. Although few trailer tires accumulate large amounts of highway miles, it's worthwhile to measure the tread and make sure the depth is not much less than a quarter of an inch. If tread depth is approaching an eighth of an inch, or if the built-in wear indicator begins to show through, it's time for replacement. On the sidewalls, check closely for signs of cracking. Long-term exposure to the sun's ultraviolet rays and ozone deteriorates tires and causes stress cracks to form in the sidewalls (see photo on page 72). These cracks are a warning sign that the tires may fail when subjected to a shock load.

When checking wear, don't forget to pay special attention to any unusual tread-wear patterns, such as excessive wear on one side or flat spots ("flat spots" sometimes occur when the trailer hasn't been moved for a long time and is more prevalent on bias ply than radial tires. In most cases, it will go away when the tire warms up on the road. If it doesn't, get rid of the tire). Tires can tell you if something is wrong. If the tread appears worn in certain places upon inspection, a possible cause is a misaligned trailer axle or an unbalanced trailer tire. Excessive vibration when under way has also been linked to a poorly aligned axle.

Before moving on, make sure that all the wheels have a full complement of lug nuts and all are wrenched tight. Now, check the wheel

Again, don't forget to check the spare.

rims for signs of rust and dents. If there is evidence of corrosion, scrape the area with a wire brush and touch up with anticorrosion paint. If the rim has a dent that appears to interfere with proper tire seating, it's best to replace it. Again, don't forget to check the spare. If this all starts to sound familiar, it's because many of these maintenance checkpoints are also part of the checklist you should use before every trip. Remember: know before you tow.

WHEEL BEARINGS

Without wheel-bearing protectors, trailer boaters would be required to dismantle the hubs and repack the bearings with grease (or oil) every time the wheels are immersed. (For most of us, that means every time the boat is used.) Fortunately, modern trailers are equipped with a bearing protector, which greatly reduces maintenance (refer to the section on wheel bearings in Chapter 2). If the trailer doesn't have bearing protectors, the best advice is to buy them as soon as possible. It's an investment that will save hours of maintenance duty.

The first thing to do in routine bearing maintenance is to jack up each trailer wheel so that it can spin freely. If there is no noise, the bearings are probably working as intended. But also take a look to see if the grease seals are holding. A small oil film is normal around the seal area, but it shouldn't be excessive. If it is, the seal may be worn. Replacement of a bad seal requires removing the complete hub assembly. If you are doing this, replace the seals with double-lipped seals. These will provide more protection from water and dirt than single-lipped seals. Pay special attention to seals on brake axles. Oil that leaks onto the brake drums adversely affects the linings.

For routine bearing-protector maintenance, press the edge of the spring-loaded piston inside the cap to see if it will move or rock. If it will, then it's still filled with grease and no action is required. If it doesn't rock, then it's fully depressed and needs grease. To refill the bearing protector with grease, push the end of a cartridge-type grease gun over the bearing protector's refill fitting, which is located in the center of the cap. Then, squeeze until the spring is fully extended. This inspection should be performed during every trip, if needed. One final tip: to keep off dirt and grime, buy a plastic cover to fit over any bearing protector that doesn't already have one.

BRAKES

Trailer brakes, especially surge brakes, are not self-adjusting. Fortunately, the adjusting process is fairly simple. First, raise the wheel off the ground. Then, remove the dust grommet from the adjusting slot. It's located on the lower part of the backside of the brake assembly. Now, insert a brake-adjusting tool into the slot and move it toward the top of the drum. This action rotates the adjustment cog. At this point, rotate it as far as it will go so that the brake shoes inside the drum are fully tightened. Now, back off the shoes by reversing the rotation of the cog. This should be done to exact specifications found in your owner's manual. Backing off five to ten notches, or when the wheel begins to turn freely, is a typical recommendation.

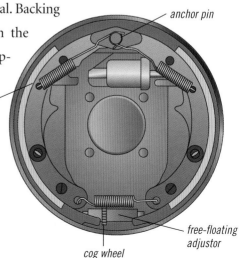

anchor pin

shoes

cog wheel

free-floating adjustor

Insert the dedicated brake-adjusting tool into the adjusting slot found on the bottom of the back side of the brake plate. Rotate the cog wheel by moving the handle of the adjusting tool in an up and down motion.

After replacing the grommet, move on to the remaining trailer wheels. Make sure all brakes are set to the same adjustment point. Then examine the shoes and lining for signs of wear. Replace as necessary. This procedure should be performed annually. If you're not comfortable performing this or any technical task in this section, go to a good service shop. Too many things can go wrong if you are just guessing during maintenance.

One popular accessory is a washdown or flush kit, which uses a garden hose and flushes out salt water from brakes as well as the trailer frame.

Flush kits are a must if you use drum brakes in salt water. Many new trailers come equipped with flush capability in which a garden hose is attached once the boat is out of the water. This protects the brakes from corrosion. If you have the hubs off, coat the moving parts with grease or oil, but be careful not to get any on the brake shoes or inside the drum.

If your trailer has disc brakes, there are a pair of areas to inspect: Brake pads will need changing, and they'll let you know the time has come by squealing whenever the brakes are applied. Rotors will need replacing when you feel a vibration or shuddering whenever depressing the brake pedal. Disc brakes cost more than drum brakes, but because there are fewer moving parts, many trailer manufacturers are moving toward making them standard on new models.

Two other areas that should be inspected are the brake lines—make sure there is no leaking of fluid and that the lines are securely attached to the trailer frame—and the master cylinder, which should be filled with brake fluid.

SUSPENSION SYSTEM

A few light duties are required to keep the suspension system in top condition. If your trailer is equipped with coil springs, torsion bars, or shock absorbers, the maintenance routine is to inspect rubber bushings, if any, to see if they're dried out, cracked, or show other signs of wear. Replace as necessary.

For leaf-spring suspensions, the end pivot points should be lubricated and all rubber bushings checked. Then make sure the steel outer surfaces of the leaves themselves aren't showing signs of serious wear. Finally, check the leaf attachment points—the hangers, shackles, equalizer bars, leaf clips, and all the attendant bolts. Replace worn parts if necessary, and make sure all screws and nuts are wrenched tight. Once-a-year attention to the suspension system should suffice.

FRAME CARE

Rust is a constant worry for those who don't own galvanized-steel or aluminum trailers. For these boaters, the best advice is to keep the trailer away from water as much as possible, and if used in salt water, rinse it off immediately after each immersion. Clean off any dirt buildup as soon as possible, since these deposits can trap moisture, and be sure to clean out deposits that work their way into open-end tubing. For painted trailers, touch up scratches immediately and apply a wax or sealer once a year. This should be done after washing it off, removing loose rust, and scraping the surface with a wire brush. Finally, give galvanized trailers an application of a corrosion-resistant coating once per season.

Another important concern for boaters is structural soundness. With the boat off the trailer, check all roller assemblies, bunks, and other frame components to see if anything looks bent or pushed out of alignment.

Shake and wiggle everything to check for sturdiness. Look for cracks, bends, or other signs of wear, especially on rubber roller bearings or keel rollers. Replace as necessary. If you have a bunk trailer, inspect the carpeting on the bunks and make sure no metal staples are coming in contact with the hull. (Some bunks are covered with carpeting that is stapled, so make a point to know this could be a potential problem area.) Carefully inspect welds, and make sure all screws and nuts are wrenched tight. Except for washing down, these duties need only be done annually.

LIGHTS AND WIRING

The biggest enemy of the trailer's electrical system is oxidation on the contact points. Caused by moisture, oxidation can result in rust or other deposits that interfere with solid electrical contacts. The best way to combat this problem is to smear a light grease on all plug prongs, receptacles, light-bulb sockets, and wire connections.

A good tip for the wiring harness plug is to scrape off all surface deposits on the prongs and in the receptacle holes, and then dab both with grease. This is especially important when storing for a long layover, but it's also a good idea for regular use. On long trips, after dabbing the plug and receptacle with grease and connecting them, it's a good idea to wrap with electrical tape to reinforce the seal.

Just as the wheel bearings heat up after a long drive, so do bulbs in the trailer's lighting system. Letting the trailer cool down for at least fifteen minutes can solve maintenance problems associated with immersing hot bulbs in cold water. If you are using LED lights, which burn cooler than the standard incandescent bulbs, the cool-down time need not be as long. It also helps to disconnect the wiring-harness plug so that the lights remain off when submerged.

Finally, make sure all connections are tightly secured, and no fraying or pinching is visible. Constant vigilance is always the best policy, but a thorough inspection of the electrical system need only be done once a year.

TONGUE COMPONENTS

First, check the coupler for rust, dents, cracks, and other signs of wear or stress. Make sure the coupler socket has maintained its shape, the ball clamp is tightly adjusted, and all screws and nuts are wrenched tight. It's also a good idea to give all pivot points and moving parts a shot of lubricating oil.

Then open the surge-brake housing and check the level of braking fluid. Refill as necessary. Lubricate pivot points, and make sure the emergency lanyard shows no signs of fraying.

Next, check the safety chains on both the tongue and winch stand. Many boaters are now using self-coiling cables which are available at most marine stores—they are preferred because they won't rust. Also, check the bow stop and the winch line. All should be closely inspected for signs of wear and replaced when necessary. Make sure all screws and nuts are wrenched tight on the winch, and lubricate moving parts for long-term protection. None of these components should ever be left unchecked for long, but detailed inspections should be done at least annually.

THE HITCH

Inspect the hitch ball for cracks and flat spots. Be sure it's wrenched tight. Then, grab the hitch and firmly shake in all directions to make sure it's solidly connected.

Now, go beneath the tow vehicle and visually check the condition of connections and welds. Make sure the hitch crossbars and connection points show no signs of serious stress, flex, or wear. Finally, check the mounting bolt holes to see if they're becoming elongated through stress. Again, constant monitoring is required for safety, but a formal inspection need only be done annually.

Again, constant monitoring is required for safety, but a formal inspection need only be done annually.

THE BOAT

As mentioned before, washing down the hull, decks, and cockpit should be done after every use, especially when the boat is used in salt water. Check the exposed surfaces for marine growth and other stains and clean them with a biodegradable hull cleaner before they become embedded. Finish with a coat of marine polish to seal the gel coat.

While you're cleaning the hull, check it for dings and cracks, and blisters or bulges, which may be signs of water migrating through the gel coat. Fixing these potentially serious problems with a fiberglass repair kit isn't as hard as you might think. Carefully drain and dry the damaged area, then patch it with epoxy-based fiberglass filler. Wait until it sets and then sand to a smooth finish. Owners of aluminum boats can bang out dings and dents with a rubber mallet, but tears and gashes may require welding.

If your boat has teak trim, clean it regularly with a nonacid cleaner. Then apply teak brightener and teak oil sealer. Padded panels and upholstered seats can be cleaned with a good vinyl cleaner and restorer.

One final tip: after every trip it's a good idea to drain, clean, and dry your marine sanitation device.

THE ENGINE

Not only are there inboard, outboard, and stern-drive engines on the market today, there are four-stroke and two-stroke models with electronic fuel injection as well. Consequently, the most important maintenance tip for any trailer-boat owner is to read the owner's manual thoroughly. A number of warnings and liabilities are involved with marine engines and you should be fully aware of them all. While this sounds intimidating, the good news is that the marine industry is building more and more user-friendly engines that, while complicated pieces of machinery and computer chips, are designed to require less and less maintenance.

> ... the most important maintenance tip for any trailer-boat owner is to read the owner's manual thoroughly.

That said, there are a number of things you can do to keep your engine running in top shape. The first is to wash down the exposed drive unit after every use. Also, it's a good idea to attach a water hose to a flushing device on an outboard or an I/O and completely flush out the raw-water cooling system. Again, these procedures are especially important after use in salt water.

Now, check the prop, skeg, and cavitation plate for dings and other signs of serious wear. Minor dings can be repaired by banging them out and filing jagged edges. Damage to a prop blade can mean damage to the prop's shock-absorber bushing, and it may require replacement. If you have a zinc anode (and you should if launching in salt water), inspect it for wear. Replace if it has deteriorated by more than 50 percent (and never paint the anode—doing so makes it useless).

Now move up to the engine and make sure all wires, electrical connections, and clamps are in good condition. Also, check the condition of the hoses for brittleness or cracking. On inboard and stern-drive engines, check the condition and tension of all drive belts. Repair or replace as necessary.

Finally, make sure all fluids—transmission fluid, battery water (if applicable), and oil are at their proper levels.

There's quite a bit more maintenance that you need to do to your engine, boat, trailer, and hitch, and this will be covered in the following section on long-term storage.

LONG-TERM STORAGE: WINTERIZING

Hibernation, or any long layover, can be just as destructive to a boat/trailer rig in the Deep South as to one in the deep freeze. Inactivity is the culprit, and if you don't prepare for it, you run the risk of incurring costly repair bills, devaluing your investment, and shortening the life of your rig. Owner manuals generally recommend that you take your rig to a service shop for prepping and a tune-up before long-term storage. However, many boaters prefer to spend a fall afternoon doing it themselves. Starting with the trailer and moving up, here are some tips to make sure that when you put your rig to bed it wakes up as good as new.

Check the condition of the tires and rims as recommended earlier. One good tip to help guard against premature rusting is to remove each wheel and thoroughly scrape the rims with a wire brush. Then apply a complete coat of paint or an anticorrosion coating. Make sure to coat the rim right up to the tire bead.

Many trailer-boat owners will remove all the wheels from their trailer and store them inside a garage or out of the sun. If you do this, cover the hubs with plastic to keep moisture out. However, punch a few small holes in the bottom of the plastic to allow any condensation to drip out. Parking the trailer over concrete is also preferable to keeping it on grass because moisture can get into the trailer's frame if it sits for an extended period of time. Storing your trailer without wheels is also an excellent deterrent to theft.

In addition to making sure the bearing protectors are full of grease, conventional wisdom calls for trailer bearings to be disassembled and repacked with grease about every 2,000 miles. The best time to do this is before a long layover. The messy job involves jacking up the trailer, removing the bearing protector, removing the wheel and hub, removing the inner and outer bearing assemblies to expose the bearing rings, replacing worn parts, cleaning all the components with solvents, and then packing the bearings with grease before reassembling. Note that the rear bearing seal will most likely be damaged during disassembly, so be prepared to install a new one before you start. If you routinely use a good-quality lubricant and maintain proper levels through the season, you may be able to skip this duty every other season, especially if the grease doesn't appear to be contaminated or to have broken down during a visual inspection. This can be a time-consuming job, so plan on spending at least one hour per wheel to perform the job correctly. Or take the trailer to a professional you trust to do the job.

As mentioned earlier, manual brake inspection should be done once a year. The same is true for checking the condition of brake shoes and linings. While disassembled, scrape out all rust and replace worn parts as necessary. In addition, now is a good time to check that the hydraulic fittings are secure. If you find any leaks, or if the brake-fluid level in the reservoir is lower than the master-cylinder ports, or if any component of the brake's hydraulic system has been disconnected during regular maintenance, the system must be bled, because air is very likely inside the brake line.

To bleed hydraulic brakes, connect a rubber hose to the bleeder fitting and submerge the free end in a container holding new brake fluid. By submerging the hose you ensure that no air is returned to the system. Then loosen the bleeder screw and pull the breakaway lanyard on the surge actuator. Make sure the master cylinder is filled during this procedure. Bleeding is completed when expelled brake fluid is free of air bubbles. To finish up, close the bleeder screw securely, remove the hose, and refill the master cylinder.

Thorough attention must be paid to the frame, bunks, rollers, suspension and electrical systems, tongue components, and the hitch before layover. Care of these parts is covered earlier in this chapter. Remove the hitch ball and store it indoors for complete protection. One additional layover tip is to spray moisture-dispersing oil on the hitch assembly, winch, leaf springs, and undercarriage assemblies.

Your boat should be stored in absolutely clean condition, since any dirt or stain will become embedded during storage. As mentioned earlier, use a biodegradable hull cleaner

Your boat should be stored in absolutely clean condition . . .

and then finish with a coat of marine polish to seal the gel coat. Repair all blisters, water bulges, dings, and cracks as necessary, and perform touch-up work on dock rash (where the hull has pressed against the dock over a period of time) and other bruises. Also, check all deck hardware for signs of wear. Repair as necessary.

If your boat spends a good portion of the summer season in a dockside slip, now is the time to apply a good coat of antifouling paint. Finally, remove the drain plugs and flush out the bilge area, livewells, baitwells, and freshwater system. Drain all thoroughly. Before covering, don't forget to open all hatches and doors.

Teak trim, upholstery, and the marine sanitation device (be it a porta potty or a head) require the attention mentioned earlier. If your boat is equipped with a head or a shower, the system must be completely flushed out, drained, and then filled with water-system antifreeze. Now is also a good time to vacuum all carpeting.

Wash the outdrive portion of your engine and flush the raw-water cooling system as indicated above. Drain and dry thoroughly. Check the prop, cavitation plate, and skeg as recommended earlier. Remove the prop and store it in a locking compartment in the boat. Finish up the prop shaft by spraying the splines and exposed components with a light grease for corrosion protection.

Now, remove the oil fill and vent plug from the lower unit and drain the oil. Inspect for metal filings, a milky color, or a burnt appearance. These signs indicate problems that need further attention at your service shop. If all looks fine, inject gear case lubricant into the lower fill hole until lube appears at the top port. Inspect the zinc anodes for wear. Carefully placed zinc anodes are used to prevent natural electrolysis that occurs when dissimilar metals are immersed in water. If they appear to be reduced in size, replace them.

Owners of inboard-equipped boats need to look beneath the hull and inspect the driveshaft packing, propeller, and rudder. Tightening the packing should be done only when the boat is in the water, so this becomes a job for the spring. Check the condition of the rudder and steering assembly and make sure all fasteners are secured. Remove the prop using water-dispersing oil (such as WD-40).

Before moving to the engine, lubricate the driveshaft, engine coupler spline, U joint, hinge pins, pinion gears, swivel pin, gimbal bearing, steering cable ram, and trim/tilt assembly using greases that are specifically formulated for each area. This is also the time to fill your power/tilt trim reservoir, and to drain water out of the speedo pickup. Use touch-up paint on exposed metal surfaces to halt the onset of rust, but make sure you don't coat the zinc anodes—that renders them useless. Outboards and I/Os should be stored in the full trim-down position to prevent strain on the hydraulic cylinder seals.

After performing the engine inspection suggested earlier regarding wires, electrical connections, hoses, clamps, and belts (note that tension should be loosened during long-term storage), it's time to clean and examine the flame arrestor (on inboards and I/Os), fuel-line screen, fuel filter, and oil filter. Replace as necessary.

Top off the fuel tank and add fuel stabilizer to prevent internal gumming as the fuel slowly breaks down into harmful resins during storage. You can also add a fuel filter absorber to your topped-off tank to remove moisture that forms through condensation, and then pour an additive that coats internal engine parts with corrosion inhibitors. But before you do any of this, check the engine owner's manual.

Change the engine oil by draining it while the engine is still warm. To fully remove all remnants of old oil in I/Os and outboards, use a hand pump hooked up through the dipstick hole. Top off the oil reservoir and add oil stabilizer to prevent viscosity changes. When replacing the oil filter, be sure to prefill it with oil so that the engine has an immediate supply of lubricant upon starting.

Now run the engine briefly to disperse the protectants throughout the engine systems. Remember that you need to use a flushing system to keep water in the cooling system whenever you run a marine engine on land. Also, keep the transmission in neutral and remove the prop to avoid danger of spinning blades.

Just before the final engine shutdown (if applicable), spray fogging oil through the carburetor intake. This should be done after the fuel line has been disconnected and the engine is about to burn up its available supply of fuel. After the engine cools down, remove the old spark plugs and spray fogging oil into the cylinders. Then crank the engine with one or two bursts to spread the oil on the cylinder walls. Install new, correctly gapped plugs if necessary.

Finally, spray all the exposed engine assemblies and surfaces with moisture-dispersing oil, and then top off power-steering, transmission (for inboards), and battery fluids. Outboard motors will completely self-drain of coolant when you trim them all the way down, but inboards and I/Os require removal of drain plugs on the engine block. Make sure all water is drained from the exhaust manifolds, exhaust risers, oil cooler, and water pump. An increasingly recommended alternative to draining is to pump environmentally approved antifreeze through the raw-water pickup. However, if you completely drain your coolant system, replace the water pump impeller when the boat is put back in service in the spring.

Don't forget to check the condition of your battery cables and terminals. Scrape off all deposits and dab with grease for protection. To maintain battery life, it's a good idea to remove it and store in a cool, dry location.

Now you're ready to close up the boat under a canvas or plastic cover. First remove all pieces of electronic equipment, trolling motors, and so forth. To protect the terminal ends, spray with a little silicone and cover with tape to prevent corrosion. On inboards only, plug the exhaust pipes to keep out moisture.

Then, bring in all canvas or fabric-covered items that are removable and wash off mildew, if any. Also spray zippers and snaps with a light lubricant to prevent rust. To prevent mildew during storage, coat canvas, plastic, upholstery, and carpeting with a mildew-control spray (available at marine

Don't underestimate the importance of covering boat. During layovers a cover protects the upholstery from sun and rain On the road it helps improve fuel economy.

centers as well as hardware stores). Coat the boat cover with a waterproofing fabric treatment. If your canvas cover comes with a center pole to promote water runoff, make sure to use it. Don't forget to tie down the cover securely, to leave ventilation holes, and to place pads beneath lines and other points that may chafe the hull.

If you are storing the boat and trailer outside your home, park the trailer so that its tongue is facing away from the street. This makes it difficult for a potential thief to do his work. Secondly, keep the boat and trailer away from tree branches. A winter storm or a heavy snow always presents the possibility of a tree limb crashing to the ground. Keep your boat out of its path.

If you are keeping the wheels on the trailer during the layover, chock the wheels. If you are taking the wheels off, set the axles on blocks and be sure to block the trailer tongue and the back end of the trailer. If possible, set the trailer so that the boat's bow is pointing up a few degrees to allow water that may collect inside to drain out. Finally, visit your rig occasionally to check on its hibernation.

In the spring, your engine should start right up after the battery is charged. First give the engine and drive a complete visual inspection, and top off the fuel tank with some fresh fuel if it's needed (fuel can evaporate over a period of time). One good tip to remember is to hook up a flushing device and run the engine to burn out the protectants before heading out. It will save you a potentially embarrassing surprise on the water.

REVIEW

1 Tires are affected by exposure to the sun, moisture, and ozone, besides wear from highway travel. Look for spider cracks in the sidewalls, uneven or worn tread, and know the proper PSI for the tires.

2 Wheel bearings are lubricated with grease or oil and the rear seals should be checked for evidence of leaks after every immersion. If replacement is necessary, insist on using double-lipped seals because they provide more protection from water and dirt, and are more durable. If oil or grease appears white, this is an indicator of water being present. Change the bearing immediately. Bearing protectors should be a part of your trailer rig.

3 Trailer brakes are either surge or electric. While many trailer manufacturers use drum brakes, disc brakes are becoming more and more popular because they have fewer moving parts. If you are uncomfortable doing an annual brake inspection yourself, this is the moment to take the trailer to a professional.

4 Inspect the leaf springs or torsion axles of your trailer for wear. Leaf springs have bushings on either end, which will eventually wear out. If this happens, you need to replace them. Coating the leaf springs with a layer of grease is also suggested as a way to prevent corrosion. Torsion axles are self-contained. If a problem occurs, the entire axle must be replaced.

5 The trailer frame is susceptible to corrosion if it isn't built with galvanized steel or aluminum. If your trailer is steel, inspect the frame for areas that require repainting. This is where corrosion can begin. Inspect bunks for torn carpeting or cracked boards (cypress is a good wood to use if a bunk requires replacement). Inspect roller assemblies for any bent parts or cracked rollers.

6 If your trailer uses incandescent lighting, inspect the bulbs after long periods of inactivity (the average life for a bulb is 15,000 hours). Check connections and inspect the wiring that runs along the trailer frame for loose fasteners, as well as frayed or damaged wire covering. Inspect the lights to ensure they are pointing in the proper direction.

7 Inspect the trailer coupler and make certain the ball clamp remains secure. Open the surge-brake housing and check the brake-fluid level. Look at the safety chains to determine if any corrosion is evident. Inspect the shackles that hold the chains (or cable) to the trailer and tow vehicle.

8 Ensure the hitch ball is wrenched tight and inspect that the hitch connection points are secure and show no stress cracks or wear.

9 Wash the boat (and trailer) immediately after use to remove salt water as well as any aquatic nuisance species that may have attached themselves to the trailer or hull. While this should be done at the boat ramp, not all facilities have washdown areas. Make it a routine job at home.

10 Properly prepare the boat and trailer for winter storage. If possible, remove the trailer tires, remove the drain plug, cover the boat, and remove valuable electronic equipment, including the battery.

CHAPTER 8

Accessories

EVERY YEAR, YOU'RE GOING TO SEE A NEW ACCESSORY at a marine center or boat show, or hear about one in an online boating bulletin board. And every year, you're going to be tempted. While most of the gear being offered/pushed/promoted falls into the "optional" category, some of it can be worthwhile for safe trailer boating. Seasoned boaters call these "essential accessories." They are the tools you'll need for routine road maintenance, water operation, unexpected emergencies, and ongoing and seasonal maintenance.

GEARING UP THE BOAT

Next to having the proper (and up-to-date) state registration numbers on the hull (and supporting information such as insurance and registration papers on board), the most important item you need for your boat is a fully outfitted Coast Guard safety package. This is a legally required set of gear that begins with personal flotation devices (PFDs) for each person aboard and a throwable float for boats longer than 16 feet. For boats less than 16 feet long, you must carry either one PFD or a throwable float for every person aboard. If your boat is longer than 16 feet, you must also carry a visual distress signal such as handheld or rocket flares fired from a pistol. Finally, all boats longer than 16 feet, except nonpowered open vessels, must carry a fire extinguisher and a horn, whistle, or bell.

As part of the required Coast Guard safety package for boats, there must be at least one PFD on board per passenger, plus one throwable float. Children under age 12 must always wear a life jacket when the boat is under way.

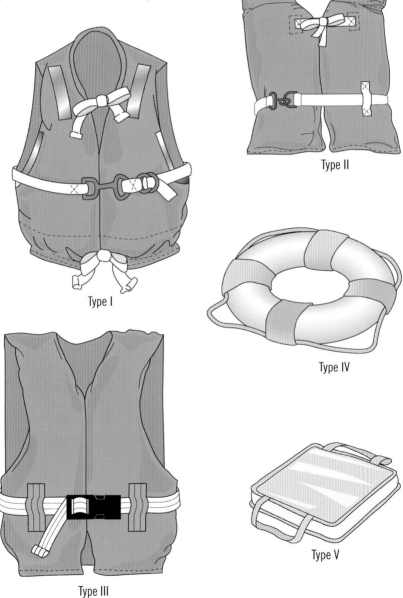

Type I

Type II

Type III

Type IV

Type V

You can either spread out the Coast Guard safety gear among several stowage compartments or keep it all together in a bag for easy accessibility. Be sure to read the labels on the fire extinguisher and flares at the start of each season and replace them before the expiration date.

Carrying an anchor isn't a Coast Guard requirement, but it's highly recommended. In addition to enabling you to tie up in a desired location, an anchor can be helpful in emergencies (your engine quits and the current or tide is running). It will hold you in place until assistance arrives or, better yet, the engine starts. Make sure you get sturdy anchor line and a chain or rode if you intend to use it frequently. Also, make sure the length of line (the scope) is sufficient for the size of the boat and depth of the water. In most cases a 7:1 scope is best—determine the water depth and multiply it by 7 and that's the length of anchor line to deploy.

For boaters who launch in the ocean or on large lakes and rivers, a VHF radio is the most important piece of electronic equipment you can have onboard. In fact, don't even consider it an accessory. Either a permanently installed unit or a portable handheld model will work, although a fix-mount VHF connected to a high-gain antenna will have a better range than a handheld. New VHF designs include the DSC (digital service calling) feature that will contact the Coast Guard using Channel 70 with the push of a button. DSC will provide the Coast Guard with your 9-digit preregistered MMSI (marine mobile service identity) number containing your name, the boat's description, and emergency contact numbers for family members. If the radio is attached to a GPS, it will also provide your waypoints in the transmission. DSC is scheduled to be in place by 2007.

A canvas or polyethylene boat cover is also an important accessory. Not only will it protect your boat from the elements—both the destructive summer sun and the harsh winter cold—but it will also prevent your rig

A properly tied-down boat cover will actually help improve gas mileage on your tow vehicle during long road trips.

from becoming a wind trap while riding down the highway. A properly tied-down boat cover will actually help improve gas mileage on your tow vehicle during long road trips.

When buying a cover, make sure you pre-measure your boat and buy one that's a good fit. You will encounter problems if your cover is either too large or too small. Fortunately, many cover manufacturers pattern their products to boatbuilder specifications.

When it comes time to put your rig in long-term storage, your boat cover should be prepared to deal with harsh conditions. Chief among them is the stress of sagging that results from puddling rainwater. To prevent this situation from turning into a destructive leak, you can create a support structure beneath the cover to promote runoff and reduce sagging. One method is to use lengths of nylon web strap to run from bow to transom. By running up and over the windscreen, the straps make sure that the cover doesn't sag. Another method involves the use of telescoping rods to create a self-supporting structure in the cockpit of the boat and in the bow, if necessary.

In addition to the rope that's used to pull the boat cover tight, it's a good idea to run several lengths of line loosely on top of the cover for extra wind protection. One line each should go over the bow, the stern, and amidships. Special nylon web straps with hook ends and ratchet buckles are built for this purpose. However, sturdy rope will work just fine for long-term storage. For wind protection during high-speed trailering, web straps are better.

TRAILER ACCESSORIES

All trailers should be equipped with a tongue jack. If yours isn't, or if you have a simple dropleg jack with a steel foot, you may want to consider upgrading to a swivel jack fitted with a dolly wheel. The dolly wheel enables you to move the trailer around easily during the hookup process. The swivel mechanism enables the jack to swing up and out of the way. Another benefit of the swivel jack is that the dolly wheel doesn't have to be removed and stored—and possibly lost or forgotten—when not in use.

Trailer boaters may occasionally find it necessary to change a flat tire on a fully loaded trailer, and to do this you need a heavy-duty trailer jack. There's an interesting new jack on the market with no moving parts: It's a D-shaped, one-piece unit that is placed beneath the axle. When you drive the trailer forward, the jack grips the road and rotates upward until it stands on end. The simple unit has a two-ton capacity and is so small and light-weight that it's easily stowed.

As mentioned earlier, wheel-bearing protectors are invaluable maintenance savers, especially if you immerse the trailer wheels during launching or do some of your boating in salt water. If your trailer isn't equipped with wheel-bearing protectors, it's highly recommended that you get them. Several brands come with see-through caps for easy lubricant-level inspection. Some have an automatic level indicator that recedes or pops out depending on the amount of grease in the cap. And a few models have pressure-release mechanisms that allow excess lubricant to gradually escape through the rear seal before damage can occur. The latest accessory for wheel bearings is the oil-bath hub, which has been discussed earlier. Like some of the grease hubs, oil-bath hubs have a see-through indicator for easy inspection of oil levels. A number of trailer manufacturers are moving toward equipping all their models with oil-bath hubs because they run cooler and require less maintenance.

There's also a hub system that allows you to repack the bearings with lubricant without disassembling the wheel bearings. When it is installed, a special fitting is located in the seal of the rear bearing. By forcing new lubricant into the rear seal, you expel the old grease and replace it with a fresh supply. For simple replenishing, you use a grease fitting (referred to as a "zerk") in the center of the front bearing cap as you would in a typical unit.

Finishing up with the wheel bearings, make sure yours are covered with a double-lip dust cap (don't confuse this with our earlier mention of a double-lip seal for the bearings—they are two different things). You might also consider buying a set of full-wheel hubcaps, which not only look good but also add a measure of protection.

Smart trailer boaters know that not all service stations stock trailer tires, so they carry a spare (and be sure it is a spare designed for a trailer and not a "spare" automobile tire). The best place to store it is on the trailer itself, typically on the tongue. The simplest mounting unit is similar to a hanging U bolt. It positions the spare tire horizontally beneath the trailer.

Trailer Tire Space Mounts
Using a high-mount bracket puts the spare tire out of the way next to the hull.

A simple low-mount bracket positions it on the trailer tongue.

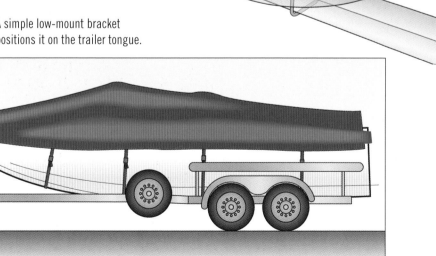

To position the tire vertically on the trailer tongue or winch stand, you can't install a high-mount carrier.

If your trailer doesn't have water-sealed submersible tail and sidelights, it's probably a good investment to install them. Even if you routinely unplug the tow-vehicle/trailer electrical connection before launching to prevent shorting out, cold water and hot lights don't mix. In the long run, submersible light fixtures are maintenance savers. Give thought to light emitting diodes (LED) lights, which operate at cooler temperatures than their incandescent counterparts.

Tie-downs, similar to the nylon web straps previously mentioned in connection with the boat cover, are important safety elements on the trailer itself. Equipped with hook ends and ratchet buckles to take in slack, tie-downs are always used to keep the boat in place on the trailer while traveling. They run from the trailer frame to several key attachment points—the transom lifting hooks, the bow eye, and even to cleats on the gunwales. They can be used to secure the battery and gas tank. One tie-down tip: If your tie-down comes in contact with the boat, insert a pad to protect the gel coat from chafing.

Ratchet-buckle tie-down straps easily and efficiently secure the boat to the trailer by fastening to transom hooks.

Other helpful trailer accessories include a power winch for heavy boats; a tongue walk ramp to provide sure footing during launching and retrieval; and trailer guides, to make it easy to position your boat on the trailer when hauling out.

TOW-VEHICLE EQUIPMENT

Probably the most important accessory for your tow vehicle is a set of large extended mirrors. By law, in most states, you must have mirrors on both sides of the vehicle that extend beyond the width of the trailered load. To improve sight lines on the right side of your rig, a stick-on convex mirror is highly recommended.

Two other useful accessories are mud flaps, to prevent road debris from damaging the hull, and a hitch-ball cover, to ward off rust when not trailering.

Two less common accessories that trailer boaters might find useful are hitch guides, which enable drivers to perform solo hookups to their trailer with the tow vehicle, and a unique universal hitch that's equipped with three different-size hitch balls.

The most popular hitch-guide design on the market consists of a base plate that's permanently installed on the back bumper. Two removable plates then fit on the base and form a capture area to guide the coupler to the hitch ball.

A more high-tech system that is common in the world of recreational vehicles is based on electronic radar guidance principles. Two receivers installed on the rear bumper of the tow vehicle receive signals from a removable transmitter that's placed on the trailer tongue. A display monitor on the tow-vehicle dash indicates the location of the coupler in relation to the hitch ball. When the signals merge together, the coupler and hitch ball are properly aligned. Generally speaking, most trailer boaters do without these toys by getting a friend or family member to stand at the rear of the vehicle and give hand signals.

The other unique product of interest to serious towers is the multiball hitch platform that inserts to a standard hitch receiver box. It's fitted with three different hitch balls (1⅞ inches, 2 inches, and 2⁵⁄₁₆ inches) and allows towers to go from one size to the other by simply rotating the unit in the receiver. For trailer boaters who also tow recreational vehicles or horse trailers, this three-in-one unit eliminates the need to carry multiple receiver-type hitch platforms.

MARINE ENGINE GEAR

The foremost accessory a trailer boater can buy for an outboard or stern-drive engine is a transom saver that helps support the lower unit during highway travel. For outboards, a hard rubber or aluminum brace is commonly used. It has a padded V-shaped yoke that's placed beneath the outboard gear case. The other end attaches to the trailer. The brace or bracket acts as an absorber of shock loads and relieves the stresses of downward force on the transom and trim/tilt seals. To accomplish this benefit for stern-drive engines, two nylon web straps can be run on either side of the lower unit from the transom to the trim/tilt rams. Should you choose not to use the "transom saver," as it's commonly called, most trailer experts suggest having the outboard in the down position, so long as it clears bumps in the road and rough pavement.

Just as the smart tower will carry a spare trailer tire, the smart boater will carry a spare prop. But stainless-steel props, which are recommended for their efficient delivery of power, are fairly expensive, so trailer boaters might want to consider carrying a prop made of composite plastic. These props are becoming more common for everyday use, and they will get you back to shore in an emergency. They're also lightweight and relatively inexpensive.

LOCKS AND ALARMS

Many boaters may not realize this but police and insurance statistics suggest the prime target boat for bandits is one on a trailer that's 18 to 26 feet long. While outside of the police statistical range, a Florida man recently had his PWC and trailer stolen from his front yard. He was able to recover both a few weeks later after seeing his PWC on his trailer in an eBay posting. He arranged with the "seller" to buy it back with the police observing the transaction.

The first line of defense in your battle with marine bandits is a variety of locks, which are now available for virtually every component of your trailer rig.

For your coupler, there's a lock that attaches to the release/lock latch. It works by preventing the lever from opening. This kind of lock can be used when the trailer is hooked to the tow vehicle, and is useful for short-term layovers. Another effective lock fastens over the hitch pin and prevents thieves from simply removing it and driving away with your hooked-up hitch platform, coupler lock, and all. Another lock that prevents thieves from driving away with your trailer is one that covers the entire coupler socket from the underside.

An effective trailer-wheel-locking device is a clamp or cuff that covers the hub so that the wheel can't be removed. Similar to a boot that's used by some local police departments to immobilize cars, this security measure can be created in a homemade version by running a chain or heavy-duty cable or length of pipe through the wheels, and then joining it together with a sturdy lock. Both of these locks are useful for long-term storage.

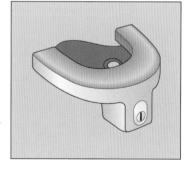

By using a simple padlock, a boater can make sure the coupler will not operate for a bandit not possessing a key.

Chief among bandits' most highly prized treasures is the boat's valuable engine or outdrive. Transom bolt locks that fit in overmounting bolts are the best way to foil them. Once installed, a collar spins uselessly around the bolts to prevent them from being loosened. Another kind of lock for outboard motors is one that fits over the entire mounting clamp.

A new generation of locks is also made for props, tires, trolling motors, and electronic instruments. These locks are ideal for short-term

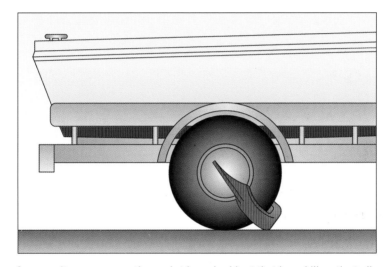

One security accessory on the market is a wheel boot that immobilizes the trailer.

storage, but for long-term security the wiser course is to remove your valuable equipment and store it away from the trailer.

In addition to locks, alarms are another major category of security accessories. Electronic alarms are intended primarily for boaters who keep their rigs in the water for a large part of the season.

A typical alarm system operates on either dockside power or battery power. Once activated, it prevents the engine from starting and sounds an alarm, which can be the boat's horn or an optional siren. The alarm is triggered when a sensor connection—a magnet and a switch—is broken.

THEFT-PREVENTION TIPS

Low-tech theft prevention measures can also be effective.

• Never park a trailered boat in a dark, secluded location. Make sure the site is well lit whether at home, the marina, or a motel. Remember: light is a boat thief's enemy.

• Back up the trailer against a building, fence, wall, tree, or other immovable object whenever possible. This restrictive placement, with the trailer remaining hooked up to the tow vehicle, will hamper a thief's ability to maneuver.

• If a boat is stored on land in the off season, remove the trailer tires and set the frame on blocks. Make potential thefts labor intensive. Thieves don't like having to work too hard at their profession.

• Remove the license plate from the trailer. If the trailer is stolen, a policeman may stop the perpetrator to check on the infraction and make inquiries.

• Remove spark plug wires if the boat is left unattended in the water for long periods.

• Use a steering-wheel lock on the boat.

• Remove all electronic equipment, props, water skis, and other costly accessories whenever the boat is left unattended, even overnight.

• Have your boat/engine/trailer serial numbers in a file so you can provide police with as much identifying material as possible. Some trailer boaters will put specific markings on the trailer frame so that it can be ID'd. Others, who obviously aren't concerned about matching colors in their rig, will paint the trailer a bright pink so that it will stand out while on the highway. It goes without saying, a thief isn't apt to pull away with a shocking-colored trailer that will force second and third looks as it travels down the road.

Sensors are typically mounted on hatches, engine covers, doorways, outboard motors, and electronic instruments. Some units trigger strobe lights as well. Among the best are those that use no electricity until triggered and shut off after a few minutes.

A recent state-of-the-art alarm system uses an onboard computer. It not only empties the bilge when necessary and recharges the batteries, but also monitors sensor signals and triggers onboard security measures. These include sounding alarms, locking the engine, and phoning in a computer message to your home or the marina office. This pricey unit requires a modem, a cell phone, and a digital communicator.

TOOLS

No trailer boater should embark on any trip without a basic toolbox that contains a couple of screwdrivers (straightedge and Phillips), a wrench set, a hammer, pliers, a knife, wire cutters, duct tape, and so forth. In addition to these tools, it's a good idea to carry a trailer jack, a complete tire-changing kit including extra lug nuts and a lug wrench, extra fuses, incandescent trailer lightbulbs (if applicable), and oil.

Less obvious but highly recommended traveling items include a tow strap, a tire-inflation gauge, a flat-tire repair kit, a prop wrench, a grease gun, extra rope, a flashlight, wooden blocks to use as wheel chocks and, if there's room, a piece of plywood that can act as a base on which a jack can be set if working in mud or sand.

Other gear and tools that are important but may not be required on every trip include motor flushers or earmuffs that connect to the water inlets on outboards and I/Os, an oil-drain pump (electric or manual) that connects to the dipstick tube, a wire brush, touch-up paint and brushes for the trailer and engine lower unit, a hydraulic brake adjusting tool, a current tester for troubleshooting problems with your trailer's lighting system, and a tongue dolly with a tilt handle and hitch ball that can be used conveniently to move a fully loaded trailer.

The most important thing to remember about trailering a boat is that, with preparation, knowledge, and the right equipment, you can go anywhere and do anything.

REVIEW

1 Your boat must have a Coast Guard-approved Type I, Type II, or Type III life jacket (personal flotation device) for every person onboard. In addition, you will need a sound-producing device (a horn either handheld or part of the permanent cockpit arrangement), a Type B-1 or Type B-2 fire extinguisher and flares. Specific information on these safety devices can be found at the Coast Guard Auxiliary website (www.cgaux.org).

2 Properly displaying the boat's identification numbers on the hull is necessary. In addition, carry insurance information and registration papers.

3 Carry a spare tire for your trailer. Manufacturers rarely offer this accessory as standard. Make sure you have jacks that will fit the trailer.

4 Trailer tie-downs are attached at the transom as well as the gunwales. They use ratchet buckles for securing the boat to the trailer. If any tie-down attachment point is stressed or if the actual tie-down shows wear, replace immediately. Inspect that the tie-down doesn't come in contact with the hull. If it does, a pad can be inserted to protect the gel coat.

5 A walk ramp on the trailer is an accessory that allows you to move about the trailer when it's in the water without getting wet while securing or releasing the boat.

6 A set of large extended mirrors will assist the tow-vehicle driver to see the trailer while on the road. Check your state laws: extended mirrors may be required.

7 You can prevent theft with a hitch lock, a wheel boot that immobilizes the trailer, and transom bolts that will lock the outboard so that it can't be removed.

8 Carry a tool kit that includes a wrench set, a variety of screwdrivers, duct tape, extra fuses, lightbulbs, and a tire-changing/repair kit.

9 Consider a transom saver to secure your outboard in the up position for highway travel.

10 A trailer-tongue dolly for moving the trailer in tight spaces (e.g., a garage) is a valued piece of equipment.

Glossary of Boating Terms

axle ratio—The relationship between the revolutions of the drive shaft and the axle (in rear-wheel drive) or the transaxle (in front-wheel drive). The figure is expressed in a ratio, for example 3.72:1, which means that there are 3.72 revolutions of the drive shaft for each revolution of the axle.

ball mount platform—The part of the hitch on which the hitch ball is mounted. Also called the hitch bar or the shank.

beam—The dimension of a boat that's measured at the hull's widest point.

belted bias tires—A type of tire that's similar to a diagonal bias tire with the addition of several plies of fabric that run through the tread area.

bow—The forward point of the boat.

bow eye—A steel hook located on the bow.

bow stop—Rubber blocks or stops located on the winch stand.

brake drum—The exterior housing of the brake system.

brake lining—The inner part of the brake drum that the brake shoes press against.

breakaway lanyard—An emergency safety device that triggers the brakes if the trailer becomes separated from the tow vehicle.

bumper/frame-mount hitch—A hitch that's attached to both the frame and the bumper. It may negate the 5-mph shock crash absorption feature built into the bumper.

bumper hitch—A hitch that's bolted solely to the rear bumper. It's not recommended for trailer boating.

bunks—Long padded or carpeted members of the trailer bed or cradle that support the weight of the boat.

bunk trailer—A type of trailer that uses long, padded bunks to carry the load of the boat.

chine—The point on the boat's hull where the bottom and sides meet.

Class I hitch—A weight-carrying hitch designed to tow up to 2,000 pounds gross trailer weight.

Class II hitch—A weight-carrying or weight-distributing hitch designed to tow up to 3,500 pounds gross trailer weight.

Class III hitch—A weight-carrying or weight-distributing hitch designed to tow up to 5,000 pounds.

Class IV hitch—A weight-carrying or weight-distributing hitch designed to tow up to 10,000 pounds.

cleat—Hardware on the deck of a boat or on a dock that's used to tie up line.

cleating knot—A simple crossover knot that's used to secure a boat to a cleat.

Coast Guard safety package—A legally required set of gear that includes personal flotation devices for each passenger on a boat, a throwable float, visual distress signals, a fire extinguisher, and a horn, whistle, or bell.

cleats

coil spring—A steel spring that's often used in conjunction with a shock absorber in a system called a coil-over shock. More common in cars than trailers.

coupler—The end of the trailer tongue, which connects to the hitch ball.

cradle—Formed by bunks or rollers or a combination of both to support the trailer load.

cruiser—A boat that has a cabin with overnight capability.

cuddy cabin—An enclosed living or stowage area located beneath the forward deck.

deadrise—The V-angle of the hull usually measured at the transom.

deep-V hull—A wedge-shaped planing hull that has a sharp angle of deadrise.

diagonal bias tires—A type of tire characterized by reinforcing plies or layers of threaded fabric (either nylon or polyester) that crisscross through the tread area and sidewalls.

diesel—A type of fuel used in four-cycle engines that generates tremendous compression to ignite a fuel of low volatility.

direct drive—A power-delivery system that tilts the inboard engine on its mountings so that the drive shaft can run in a straight line through the bottom of the hull.

displacement hull—A type of round-bottom hull design that smoothly displaces water while under way to reduce hydrodynamic friction.

dolly wheel—A part on the end of a trailer jack that gives mobility to the tongue. Instead of dolly wheels, some jacks are equipped with stationary steel feet.

dry weight—This figure refers to the weight of the boat prior to the filling of the fuel and freshwater tanks and the installation of optional equipment and, sometimes, the engine.

fender—A metal or plastic cover that fits over the wheel of a trailer. Also, a cushion used to protect the hull of the boat when tied to a dock.

fifth-wheel hitch—A trailer hitch that's mounted in the center of a pickup truck bed.

fixed ball-mount platform—A one-piece hitch in which the hitch ball is attached to a fixed hitch platform or bar.

flatbed trailer—A type of trailer that has a flat surface made of planks, plywood, steel, or aluminum that supports the trailer load.

flat-bottom boat—A boat with a simple squared-off hull sometimes found on rowboats, johnboats, dinghies, and small sailing skiffs.

flat-V—A type of planing hull that has a shallow, nearly flat deadrise.

flushing device—A set of clamps that goes over water inlets on either side of the lower unit of an outboard or stern-drive motor. It hooks up to a garden hose and flushes out the raw-water cooling system.

flying bridge—A second-level helm area on a boat equipped with operational instrument controls.

four-cycle motor—A gasoline or diesel engine that has a power stroke once every four cycles of the piston. Inboard and stern-drive engines are typically four-cycle motors. Also called *four-stroke*.

frame-mount hitch—A hitch that's bolted or welded to the frame of the tow vehicle.

Gross Axle Weight Rating (GAWR)—The maximum allowable weight that a simple axle is designed to carry.

Gross Combined Weight Rating (GCWR)—The maximum allowable weight of the fully loaded tow vehicle and the fully loaded trailer. This figure includes all passengers and cargo.

Gross Trailer Weight Rating (GTWR)—The maximum allowable weight of the fully loaded trailer. This includes cargo. Same as GVWR.

Gross Vehicle Weight Rating (GVWR)—The maximum allowable weight of a fully loaded vehicle. This includes passengers and cargo.

guide bars—Vertical posts mounted on the sides of the trailer to help center the boat on the cradle or bed during retrieval.

gunwale—The upper edge of the side of a boat.

helm—The driver's position or control post of a boat.

hitch—The steel framework that attaches to a tow vehicle and carries the hitch ball.

hitch ball—The part of the hitch that comes in metal-to-metal contact with the coupler.

hitch bar—The part of the hitch that the hitch ball mounts on. Also called the ball-mount platform or shank.

hub—A part that enables the wheel to spin around the axle.

hull—The structural body of the boat that comes into contact with the water.

inboard motor—A type of gasoline or diesel engine that's located inside the hull.

I/O motor—Stands for inboard/outboard. *See stern-drive motor.*

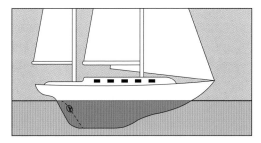

keel

keel—Located at the bottom of the centerline of a sailboat or powerboat hull. Typically, it refers to a sailboat appendage that's either retractable, which means that it can slide up and out of the way, or fixed, which means that its bulb is filled with weight to act as ballast.

keel rollers—Rubber or plastic trailer rollers that support the keel point of the hull.

leaf springs—A part of a vehicle's suspension system that's made of steel strips or leaves that flex when the wheels go over a bump.

lee side—The side of an object that's sheltered from the wind. The opposite is the windward side.

Manufacturer's Tow Package—A cluster of factory-installed trailering components that's available at the time of the tow vehicle's purchase. It can more than double the vehicle's tow rating.

marinization—The addition of marine components to inboard and stern-drive engines, which consist primarily of automotive technology.

mast—The vertical spar that supports a sail. It can be either stepped, which means that it can be easily taken down, or fixed, which means that it's permanently installed.

mod-V—A type of planing hull that has a medium angle of deadrise.

mod-VP—A type of tunnel-hull boat that has a V-bottom flanked by two sponsons. It offers the best of riding comfort and air-entrapment performance.

outboard motor—A marine engine that's bolted onto a boat's transom. Typical outboards are two-cycle or four-cycle gasoline engines. Small outboards can be portable.

outdrive—the lower unit or drive leg of a stern-drive motor.

overall length—The dimension of the boat that's measured along the centerline from the transom to the bow.

package boat—A prerigged boat, motor, and trailer package with a long list of standard equipment that's sold with few or no options.

Personal Flotation Device (PFD)—A vestlike safety jacket that aids in keeping swimmers afloat. Part of the legally required Coast Guard safety package.

Personal Watercraft (PWC)—A small, lightweight craft that's similar to a motorcycle, but operates on the water. It's generally powered by a water jet motor.

planing hull—A type of hull that's characterized by hard chines and the ability to lift partially out of the water to reduce drag.

pontoon boat—A type of boat that has twin air-tight, semidisplacement

Personal Watercraft (PWC)

hulls connected above water by a platform deck. The hulls are typically made of welded aluminum.

radial ties—A type of tire characterized by multiple plies of fabric with the cords or thread running at a 90-degree angle from the centerline.

receiver box—The part of a hitch that receives and securely holds a removable ball-mount platform or hitch bar.

receiver hitch—A hitch that has a removable ball-mount platform or hitch bar.

rim—The steel part of the wheel to which the rubber tire is mounted.

roller trailer—A type of trailer that uses rubber or plastic rollers mounted on brackets to support the trailer load.

runabout—A small, light recreational boat without overnight amenities.

safety chains—Chains that connect the trailer tongue to the tow vehicle. They secure the trailer to the tow vehicle in case the coupler detaches. Cables are also used in place of chains.

semidisplacement hull—A round-bottom hull design with soft chines. It has some planing characteristics.

shank—The part of the hitch that the hitch ball mounts on. Also called the hitch bar or hitch shank.

spindle—The part of the axle that the wheel bearings rotate around.

sponsons—The water contact points on a tunnel-hull boat.

spring line—A line that's cleated amidships on the boat or dock.

step bumper hitch—A hitch that's built into the rear bumper, typically on an SUV or pickup truck. It usually has attachment points on the vehicle frame, and if it doesn't, it's not recommended for trailer boating.

stern-drive motor—A type of marine engine that combines the best of the outboard and the inboard. The engine is mounted inboard and the drive shaft runs through a cutout in the transom to an exposed lower unit or drive leg. Most stern drives use gasoline engines. Also called I/Os.

surge brakes—A hydraulic trailer braking system that's activated by a sudden slowing of forward momentum when the tow-vehicle brakes are applied.

sway—A side-to-side wandering movement of the trailer behind the tow vehicle while under way.

sway control device—Attaches to the trailer tongue and the tow vehicle and uses friction to resist pivoting or sway movement of the trailer while driving. It is generally a quick fix that may temporarily mask the effects of a larger problem.

tandem-axle trailer—A trailer that has two axles for extra strength and stability. Also called a dual-axle trailer.

tiller-handle motor—A type of motor that requires the boater to use a control arm for steering while under way.

tilt-bed trailer—A type of trailer that has a hinged tongue or hinged frame, which enables the bed to tilt like that of a dump truck.

tiller-handle motor

tongue—*see trailer tongue.*

tongue jack—A jack mounted on the trailer tongue that raises the coupler to connect with the hitch ball.

tongue weight—The weight of the loaded trailer on the hitch. It should be a maximum of 10% of the trailer load for most applications.

torsion bar—A trailer suspension system that has a hexagonal exterior axle made of tubular steel that encloses a three-sided solid-steel shaft, which in turn is surrounded by rubber inserts. The rubber inserts absorb the twisting motion caused by the wheels going over bumps.

tow rating—The maximum amount of weight a vehicle is rated to tow.

trailer bed—Formed by a pattern of bunks or rollers or a combination of both to support the trailer load.

trailer boat—A marine craft that's generally no more than twenty-six feet long and eight feet six inches wide.

trailering height—The measurement between the ground and the bottom of the hull when it's mounted on a trailer, plus the height of the boat.

trailer tongue—The forward end of the trailer nearest the tow vehicle. The coupler and other components are mounted on the tongue.

multi-axle trailer

multi-axle trailer

tri-hull—A type of planing hull that's characterized by three V-shaped, side-by-side bottom components. Also called a cathedral hull.

trim—A boat operation term that refers to the running position of the engine's drive unit. On boats that are equipped with power trim, the drive unit can be raised or lowered by pressing a button.

tunnel-hull boat—A type of high-performance boat characterized by twin hulls that trap air and create lift for minimum drag.

two-cycle—Gasoline engine technology in which a power stroke is delivered on every other cycle of the piston. Outboards are typically two-cycle engines. Also called two-stroke.

V-drive—A power-delivery system that splits the drive shaft to form a V-angle before running the prop shaft through the bottom of the hull.

V-hull—A wedge-shaped planing hull.

weight-distributing hitch—A frame-mounted hitch that uses spring bars to apply leverage between the tow vehicle and the trailer to distribute tongue weight to all wheels of the tow vehicle.

wheel bearings—Two rings of steel rollers inside the hub that enable the wheel to rotate freely around the spindle.

wheel-bearing protectors—Caps that fit over the wheel hubs to protect the wheel bearings by keeping grease under pressure to prevent water from getting in.

winch—A manual or electric mechanism used to haul or hoist a boat.

wiring harness—The heavy-duty plug that connects the tow-vehicle and trailer electrical systems.

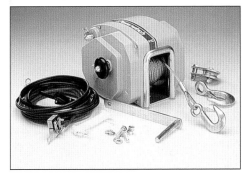

electric trailer winch

Photography Credits

Index